Wise Men Talking Series

XUN ZI
Says

荀子 说

蔡希勤 编注

□ 责任编辑 **韩颖**

□ 翻译 **张乐**

□ 绘图 **李士伋**

人家说 老系列丛书

华语教学出版社
SINOLINGUA

First Edition 2012

ISBN 978-7-5138-0142-3
Copyright 2012 by Sinolingua
Published by Sinolingua
24 Baiwanzhuang Road, Beijing 100037, China
Tel: (86)10-68320585   68997826
Fax: (86)10-68997826   68326333
http://www.sinolingua.com.cn
E-mail: hyjx@sinolingua.com.cn
Printed by Beijing Songyuan Printing Co., Ltd.

Printed in the People's Republic of China

老人家说

Wise Men Talking

俗曰:"不听老人言,吃亏在眼前。"

老人家走的路多,吃的饭多,看的书多,经的事多,享的福多,受的罪多,可谓见多识广,有丰富的生活经验,老人家说的话多是经验之谈,后生小子不可不听也。

在中国历史上,春秋战国时期是中国古代思想高度发展的时期,那个时候诸子并起,百家争鸣,出现了很多"子"字辈的老人家,他们有道家、儒家、墨家、名家、法家、兵家、阴阳家,多不胜数,车载斗量,一时星河灿烂。

后来各家各派的代表曾先后聚集于齐国稷下学宫。齐宣王是个开明的诸侯王,因纳无盐丑女钟离春为后而名声大噪。他对各国来讲学的专家学者不问来路一律管吃管住,给予政府津贴。对愿留下来做官的,授之以客卿,造巨室,付万钟;对不愿做官的,也给予"不治事而议论"之特殊待遇。果然这些人各为其主,各为其派,百家争鸣,百花齐放,设坛辩论,著书立说:有的说仁,有的说义,有的说无为,有的说逍遥,有的说非攻,有的说谋攻,有的说性善,有的说性恶,有的说亲非亲,有的说马非马,知彼知己,仁者无敌……留下了很多光辉灿烂的学术经典。

可惜好景不长,秦始皇时丞相李斯递话说"焚书坑儒",结果除秦记、医药、卜筮、种树书外,民间所藏诗、书及百家典籍均被一把火烧个精光。到西汉武帝时,董仲舒又上书提出"罢黜百家,独尊儒术",从此,儒学成了正统,"黄老、刑名百家之言"成为邪说。

"有德者必有言",儒学以外的各家各派虽屡被扫荡,却不断变换着生存方式以求不灭,并为我们保存下了十分丰富的经典著作。在这些经典里,先哲们留下了很多充满智慧和哲理的、至今仍然熠熠发光的至理名言,我们将这些各家各派的老人家的"金玉良言"编辑成这套《老人家说》丛书,加以注释并译成英文,采取汉英对照方式出版,以飨海内外有心有意于中国传统文化的广大读者。

As the saying goes, "If an old dog barks, he gives counsel."

Old men, who walk more roads, eat more rice, read more books, have more experiences, enjoy more happiness, and endure more sufferings, are experienced and knowledgeable, with rich life experience. Thus, what they say is mostly wise counsel, and young people should listen to them.

The Spring and Autumn (770–476 BC) and Warring States (475–221 BC) periods of Chinese history were a golden age for ancient Chinese thought. In those periods, various schools of thought, together with many sages whose names bore the honorific suffix "Zi," emerged and contended, including the Taoist school, Confucian school, Mohist school, school of Logicians, Legalist school, Military school and Yin-Yang school. Numerous and well known, these schools of thought were as brilliant as the Milky Way.

Later representatives of these schools of thought flocked to the Jixia Academy of the State of Qi. Duke Xuan of Qi was an enlightened ruler, famous for making an ugly but brilliant woman his wife. The duke provided board and lodging, as well as government subsidies for experts and scholars coming to give lectures, and never inquired about their backgrounds. For those willing to hold official positions, the duke appointed them guest officials, built mansions for them and paid them high salaries. Those unwilling to take up official posts were kept on as advisors. This was an era when "one hundred schools of thought contended and a hundred flowers blossomed." The scholars debated in forums, and wrote books to expound their doctrines: Some preached benevolence; some, righteousness; some, inaction; some, absolute freedom; some, aversion to offensive war; some, attack by stratagem; some, the goodness of man's nature; some, the evil nature of man. Some said that relatives were not relatives; some said that horses were not horses; some urged the importance of knowing oneself and one's enemy; some said that benevolence knew no enemy .... And they left behind many splendid classic works of scholarship.

Unfortunately, this situation did not last long. When Qin Shihuang (reigned 221–210 BC) united all the states of China, and ruled as the First Emperor, his prime minister, Li Si, ordered that all books except those on medicine, fortune telling and tree planting be burned. So, all poetry collections and the classics of the various schools of thought were destroyed. Emperor Wu (reigned 140–88 BC) of the Western Han Dynasty made Confucianism the orthodox doctrine of the state, while other schools of thought, including the Taoist and Legalist schools, were deemed heretical.

These other schools, however, managed to survive, and an abundance of their classical works have been handed down to us. These classical works contain many wise sayings and profound insights into philosophical theory which are still worthy of study today. We have compiled these nuggets of wisdom uttered by old men of the various ancient schools of thought into this series Wise Men Talking, and added explanatory notes and English translation for the benefit of both Chinese and overseas readers fond of traditional Chinese culture.

目录

CONTENTS

1

聪明君子者，善服人者也〔12〕

A wise governor knows well how to convince his people.

川渊深而鱼鳖归之〔14〕

Deep water invites fishes and turtles.

D

道存则国存，道亡则国亡〔16〕

Tao lives and the country exists. Tao dies and the country disappears.

道虽迩，不行不至〔18〕

Near as a destination is, one cannot reach it without the exertion of traveling.

道者，非天之道，非地之道，人之道也〔20〕

The Tao of the sage kings is neither the Tao of Heaven nor the Tao of Earth.

德必称位，位必称禄〔22〕

One should possess virtues proportional to one's position ...
One's position must be deserving of its payment.

德厚者进而佞说者止〔24〕

(Good governance should guarantee that) those with virtue are promoted and flatterers are dismissed.

凡得胜者，必与人也〔26〕

Those who want to win a victory must depend on the people.

凡奸人之所以起者〔28〕

The rise of evils and vices is rooted in ...

凡人有所一同〔30〕

People all share common traits.

凡用兵，攻战之本，在乎壹民〔32〕

The wholehearted support of the people is essential for the command

of an army in wartime.

非我而当者，吾师也〔34〕

Those who justifiably criticize me are my teachers.

夫贵为天子，富有天下〔36〕

To be crowned as the emperor and hold a whole country's wealth ...

父有争子，不行无礼〔38〕

In fathering an outspoken son, one will not breach etiquette.

公生明，偏生暗〔40〕

Impartiality breeds clarity and partiality obscurity.

古之学者为己，今之学者为人〔42〕

A gentleman studies for self cultivation; a petty man studies for self aggrandizement.

国危，则无乐君；国安，则无忧民〔44〕

When a state is threatened, no monarch can be at ease; when a state is at peace, its citizens will be without suffering.

国无礼，则不正〔46〕

Without etiquette there can be no orderly country.

J

积土成山，风雨兴焉〔48〕

Pile up the earth to make a mountain, which is conducive to the formation of the wind and rain.

坚甲利兵不足以为胜〔50〕

Protective armors and sharp weapons alone cannot guarantee the defeat of enemy.

见善，脩然必以自存也〔52〕

Seeing goodness, one should examine oneself and emulate such goodness.

君人者，爱民而安〔54〕

For a monarch, love for one's people will build a stable state.

君人者欲安，则莫若平政爱民矣〔56〕

If the monarch wants a turmoil free state, then nothing is more important than ruling with fairness and caring for the people.

君子隘穷而不失，劳倦而不苟〔58〕

In poverty, a gentleman will not lose his integrity; exhausted, he will be still committed to his work.

君子耻不修，不耻见污〔60〕

A gentleman will be ashamed of not cultivating himself, instead of feeling humiliated by others' insults.

君子崇人之德，扬人之美〔62〕

A gentleman will promote others' good deeds and compliment others' merits.

君子耳不听淫声，目不视女色〔64〕

A gentleman should not listen to licentious music, or stare at attractive beauties.

君子居必择乡，游必就士〔66〕

If a gentleman wants to settle down, he will certainly choose a good neighborhood in which to do so; if he is on a journey, he will surely stay close to men of insight and virtue.

君子宽而不僈，廉而不刿〔68〕

A gentleman has poise but will not indulge in idleness; he is impartial and fair but will not allow justice to inflict unwarranted harm upon others.

君子能为可贵，不能使人必贵己〔70〕

A gentleman has virtue and abilities worthy of appreciation, but he cannot claim others' recognition.

君子贫穷而志广，富贵而体恭〔72〕

In poverty, a gentleman will not be deprived of vision and an open mind; with wealth and power, he will remain polite and courteous.

君子贤而能容罢，知而能容愚〔74〕

Virtuous and able, a gentleman is able to tolerate the less able; intelligent, he is able to tolerate the less enlightened.

君子行不贵苟难，说不贵苟察〔76〕

Even if an unseemly action requires skill and ability, gentlemen will not value it; even if an indecorous doctrine contains insight, gentlemen will not appreciate it.

君子养心，莫善于诚〔78〕

As to a gentleman's self cultivation, nothing outweighs his sincerity and truthfulness.

君子役物，小人役于物〔80〕

A gentleman makes use of worldly objects, while a petty man is burdened by them.

君子易知而难狎〔82〕

A gentleman is approachable but not easy to behave towards in an indecorously familiar way.

L

力不若牛，走不若马〔84〕

(Man's) strength cannot match that of the ox and a man cannot outrun a horse.

良农不为水旱不耕〔86〕

A good peasant will not lay farming aside because of flood or drought.

流丸止于瓯臾，流言止于知者〔88〕

A rolling pellet stops in a depression; a rumor will be dispelled by a wise person.

M

马骇舆，则君子不安舆〔90〕

If the carriage horses are frightened, gentlemen in the carriage cannot ride safely.

明主尚贤能而飨其盛〔92〕

A wise monarch respects the noble and entrusts the able, and hence can share their achievements.

明主有私人以金石宝玉〔94〕

A wise monarch may bestow gold and jewelry in private ...

木受绳则直,金就砺则利〔96〕

A timber can be made straight using the ink mark left by an unbent

line; metal instruments can be made sharp through whetting.

目不能两视而明, 耳不能两听而聪〔98〕

Eyes do not see clearly when trying to focus on two points; ears

do not hear clearly if tuned to two sounds.

N

能当一人, 而天下取〔100〕

If a worthy person is appointed to office, the state will be ruled

properly.

P

蓬生麻中, 不扶而直〔102〕

If fleabane grows up in the midst of straight hemp, it will stand

erect without support.

Q

强本而节用, 则天不能贫〔104〕

Encourage farming and frugality, and Heaven will spare people

from poverty.

轻田野之税，平关市之征〔106〕

Lower the agriculture tax, and exempt the trading tax.

R

人生而有欲〔108〕

Men are born with desires.

人无法则伥伥然〔110〕

Without laws and rules, people will behave arrogantly.

人无礼，则不生〔112〕

Those who ignore etiquette will not survive.

人之情，食欲有刍豢〔114〕

It is common for people to want to have meat for food.

仁义德行，常安之术也〔116〕

Beneficence and morality is the path to long-lasting peace.

仁人之兵，所存者神，所过者化〔118〕

The army headed by a benevolent and righteous person will make where it stays a well-governed place and influence all other places it traverses.

荣辱之大分，安危、利害之常体〔120〕

The fundamental difference between honor and disgrace lies in people's attitudes towards danger and interest.

入孝出弟，人之小行也〔122〕

Obedience to one's parents and respecting the elders in a society is the most basic kind of virtue.

S

善学者，尽其理〔124〕

A good learner seeks a thorough understanding of knowledge.

伤良曰谗，害良曰贼〔126〕

Making false and malicious statements about the innocent is termed slander.

赏不欲僭，刑不欲滥〔128〕

No excessive rewards or punishments.

尚贤使能，赏有功，罚有罪〔130〕

Honor the virtuous, appoint the capable, award those with achievements, and punish the guilty.

少而不学，长无能也〔132〕

Having not studied in youth, one will not be able to fill an office in one's maturity.

身劳而心安，为之〔134〕

It is worthwhile to do things that exhaust one's body but put one's conscience at ease.

神莫大于化道，福莫长于无祸〔136〕

Wisdom is no more than conforming to the laws of nature; luck is no more than being trouble free.

声乐之入人也深，其化人也速〔138〕

Music is powerful in influencing people, and swift in moving people.

声无小而不闻，行无隐而不形〔140〕

No matter how tiny the voice is, it is still audible; no matter how secretive an action is, it is still perceivable.

施薪若一，火就燥也〔142〕

If the firewood is spread out, then fires will start where the dry wood congregates.

水火有气而无生〔144〕

Water and fire have got the rhythm of breath but have no life.

岁不寒，无以知松柏〔146〕

If it were not for the chilly season, pines and cypresses could not exhibit their character.

T

天不为人之恶寒而辍冬〔148〕

Heaven will not eschew winter because people loathe the cold.

天不言，而人推高焉〔150〕

Heaven does not speak, but people honor its highness.

天道有常：不为尧存，不为桀亡〔152〕

The course of Heaven is eternal: it does not exist for the sage kings like Emperor Yao or die due to atrocious kings like Emperor Jie.

W

为上则不能爱下，为下则好非其上〔154〕

As the superior, one cannot tend to one's subordinates if as the subordinate one slanders one's superior's.

闻之而不见，虽博必谬〔156〕

Having heard of things but not having seen them oneself, one will err even though one is well-informed.

无德不贵，无能不官〔158〕

Without virtue, one cannot deserve a high status. Without abilities, one cannot secure an official position.

物类之起，必有所始〔160〕

There must be a beginning for every single occurrence.

X

相高下，视硗肥，序五种〔162〕

In terms of identifying the terrain features and the soil quality, and scheduling the planting of five main crops . . .

相形不如论心；论心不如择术〔164〕

Observing one's physiognomy ranks lower than assessing one's thought. Assessing one's thought is of less weight than judging one's behavior.

心不使焉，则白黑在前而目不见〔166〕

Distracted, one cannot see white or black before one's eyes.

新浴者振其衣，新沐者弹其冠〔168〕

After bathing, people will shake their apparel before putting it on. After washing their hair people will beat their hat before it is donned.

选贤良，举笃敬，兴孝弟，收孤寡〔170〕

Appoint the capable and virtuous. Promote the truthful and trustworthy. Advocate obedience to one's parents and elder brothers. Take care of orphans and the widowed.

学不可以已〔172〕

Learning must be never concluded.

学者，非必为仕〔174〕

Learning is not necessarily for an official career.

Y

言必当理，事必当务〔176〕

Make appropriate remarks and manage affairs properly.

言有召祸也，行有招辱也〔178〕

Heedless utterances may spell misfortune and disaster. Imprudent actions may beget disgrace and humiliation.

以善先人者，谓之教〔180〕

Showing others good deeds is deemed teaching.

佚而治，约而详，不烦而功〔182〕

Properly govern a state with ease; give simple yet well thought out orders; make achievements in state affairs without exertion.

友者，所以相有也〔184〕

Friends are those who hold affection for each other.

有师法者，人之大宝也〔186〕

Education and laws are the most precious treasures of the people.

与人善言，暖于布帛〔188〕

Kind words are as genial as warm clothes.

乐者，圣人之所乐也〔190〕

Music is what the sages favor.

乐者，乐也〔192〕

Music is enjoyment.

Z

知莫大乎弃疑，行莫大乎无过〔194〕

No wisdom is greater than the wisdom beyond bewilderment. No meritorious action exceeds the action beyond reproach.

志意修则骄富贵；道义重则轻王公〔196〕

With a tempered will, one is able to shun power and wealth; holding one's principles dear, one can slight princes and aristocrats.

自知者，不怨人；知命者，不怨天〔198〕

Those who know their own limitations will not blame others; those who comprehend the course of fate will not blame Heaven.

足国之道，节用裕民，而善臧其余〔200〕

The approach to prospering a country lies in economic expenditure, enriching the people and the proper keeping of the surplus.

荀子说

XUN ZI SAYS

荀子,姓荀名况,字卿。战国末期赵国人。他是孔门儒家的杰出传人,是一位先进的思想家、政治家和文学家。

他五十岁始游学齐国,三为稷下祭酒,齐襄王尊为师。后遭诽议,去齐之楚,任兰陵令,后定居兰陵,著书授徒,李斯、韩非皆出其门下。他曾西游入秦,对秦首相范雎说:"佚而治,约而详,不烦而动,治之至也。"

他认为人性皆恶,不以礼义矫正之,则不能为善。只有多积善缘,才能成就功德。

他主张学者著书立说,应该推陈出新,向前发展。"君子曰:学不可以已。青取于蓝,而青于蓝;冰生于水,而寒于水。"

Xun Zi's given name was Kuang, and the name of courtesy, Qing. Xun zi was a native of the State of Zhao during the late Warring States Period (475 – 221BC). He was a pioneering thinker, statesman, and writer.

At the age of fifty, he started to travel and study in the State of Qi and taught thrice at Jixia Academy, the most famous scholarly academy in ancient China, whereupon King Xiang of Qi honored him as a teacher. Xun Zi was ultimately slandered in the Qi court, after which he retreated to the State of Chu where he was appointed Magistrate of Lanling. He settled there to write books and teach his disciples. Li Si (Prime Minister to the First Qin Emperor) and Han Fei Zi (a famed philosopher) were his most notable disciples. He once traveled west to Qin, where he advised Fan Ju, the prime minister, that "Properly govern a state with ease; give simple yet well thought out orders; make achievements in state affairs without exertion. Such are the ideals of statesmanship."

Xun Zi held that man's nature is inherently evil and argued for the use of ancient rites and regulations to guide the self towards goodness. He believed that achievements are due to the accumulation of good deeds.

He advocated that scholars should record their philosophy in books, and allow new ideas to replace old ones in the forever advancing journey of knowledge. This belief is best encapsulated in his book—"The gentleman says, 'Learning must be never concluded. Though blue comes from the indigo plant, it is bluer than indigo. Ice is made from water, but it is colder than the water from which it was formed.'"

百乐者，生于治国者也

Pleasures are born in properly governed states.

百乐者，生于治国者也；忧患者，生于乱国者也；急逐乐而缓治国者，非知乐者也。

《荀子·王霸》

Pleasures are born in properly governed states, whereas hardships are born in turbulent states. The king who is so eager to pursue pleasures as to lay aside the affairs of the state is not one who can fully appreciate the value of pleasure.

【注释】

荀子曰："故明君者必先治其国，然后百乐得其中；暗君者必将急逐乐而缓治国，故忧患不可胜校也，必至于身死国亡，然后止也。"百乐：各种快乐。百，概数。言其多，如"百家"、"百姓"、"百战百胜"。忧患：犹患难。《易·系辞下》："作易者其有忧患乎？"《孟子·告子下》："入则无法家拂士，出则无敌国外患者，国恒亡。然后知生于忧患而死于安乐也。"急：疾速。与缓慢相对。《荀子·强国》："非不以此为务也，疾养缓急之有相先者也。"

【译文】

各种快乐只发生在政治清明的国家里，各种忧患只发生在动乱不定的国家里。急于追逐快乐而放缓治理国家的君主，不是真正懂得快乐的人。

不积跬步，无以致千里

A journey of one thousand miles requires every step of the journey.

不积跬步，无以致千里，不积小流，无以成江海。骐骥一跃，不能十步；驽马十驾，功在不舍。锲而舍之，朽木不折；锲而不舍，金石可镂。

《荀子·劝学》

A journey of one thousand miles requires every step of the journey; an ocean or a river requires the convergence of every brook and stream. A swift horse cannot exceed ten paces in a single prance, yet in ten days an inferior horse could travel far. The latter's success lies in its persistence. Carve but give up halfway, and even a decayed piece of wood will not break; work with perseverance, and metal and stone alike can be engraved.

【注释】

跬步：半步。古之半步，相当于今之一步。《大戴礼·劝学》："是故不积跬步，无以致千里。" 骐骥（qíjì）：千里马。《庄子·秋水》："骐骥骅骝，一日而驰千里。" 驽（nú）马：能力低下的马。十驾：马驾车走十天的路程。马早晨驾车，晚上卸驾，因称一天的路程为一驾。故说："驽马十驾，功在不舍。"

【译文】

千里之远是一步一步走出来的；江海是一沟一溪的小水流汇聚而成。千里马一跃，也不能跳十步远；劣马跑十天，也能赶上千里马，其成功在于不放弃。镂刻半途而废，糟木头也弄不断；坚持不停止，金石也可以雕镂。

不闻，不若闻之

Not having heard is not as good as having heard.

荀子说

不闻，不若闻之；闻之，不若见之；见之，不若知之。学至于行之而止矣。

《荀子·儒效》

Not having heard is not as good as having heard; having heard is not as good as having seen; having seen is not as good as understanding; understanding is not as good as putting understanding into action. The ultimate goal of study is to put one's knowledge into practice.

【注释】

荀子说："实行是学习的最终目的。"闻：听见。《礼记·大学》："心不在焉，视而不见，听而不闻。"见：看见。《诗经·王风·采葛》："一日不见，如三秋兮。"知：知道，了解。《尚书·皋陶谟》："知人则哲。"《论语·宪问》："知我者其天乎？"行：实行。《论语·先进》："冉有问：'闻斯行诸？'子曰：'闻斯行之。'"

【译文】

没有听过，不如听到；听到不如看到；看到不如知道；知道不如实行。学以致用是学习的最高境界。

不知则问，不能则学

Ask when something is beyond one's knowledge; study when something is beyond one's ability.

不知则问，不能则学，虽能必让，然后为德。

《荀子·非十二子》

Ask when something is beyond one's knowledge; study when something is beyond one's ability; modestly let others act first even if one is qualified. Then one can become a man of virtuous and noble character.

【注释】

荀子认为君子之道应该"兼服天下之心：高尚尊贵，不以骄人；聪明圣智，不以穷人；齐给速通，不以先人；刚毅勇敢，不以伤人"。能：能够，胜任。《尚书·西伯戡黎》："乃（汝）罪多参在上，乃能责命于天？"《左传·成公十六年》："夫合诸侯，非吾所能也，以遗能者。"让：谦让，礼让。《尚书·尧典》："允恭克让。"注："推贤尚善曰让。"《礼记·曲礼上》："是以君子恭敬撙节退让以明礼。"让，谦让，儒家提倡"礼让为国"。

【译文】

不懂就问，不能胜任工作就要去学习，即使懂得也要礼让，把这作为自己品德修养的基础。

材性知能，君子小人一也

In nature and intelligence, neither the gentleman nor the petty man is superior to the other.

材性知能，君子小人一也。好荣恶辱，好利恶害，是君子小人之所同也。若其所以求之之道则异矣。

《荀子·荣辱》

In nature and intelligence, neither the gentleman nor the petty man is superior to the other. Both of them enjoy honor and loathe disgrace, favor interest and detest harm. Their difference merely lies in their approaches to pursuing honor and interest.

【注释】

材性知能：本性和智能。材，资质。《礼记·中庸》："故天之生物，必因其材而笃焉。"知（zhì），同"智"。知、智为古今字。《易·蹇》："见险而能止，知矣哉。"《论语·子罕》："择不处仁，焉得知。"《论语》"智"皆作"知"。

【译文】

本性和智能，君子和小人本没有高下之分。在好荣耀而憎恶屈辱、好利益而憎恶危害这方面，君子和小人也没有什么不同。他们只是取得荣耀和利益的方式不一样。

聪明君子者，善服人者也

A wise governor knows well how to convince his people.

聪明君子者，善服人者也。人服，而埶从之，人不服，而埶去之。

《荀子·王霸》

A wise governor knows well how to convince his people. With people's hearts, he possesses power and influence; without them, he will lose both.

【注释】

聪明：明智，明察。《尚书·皋陶谟》："天聪明，自我民聪明。"《淮南子·脩务》："谓一人聪明而不足以遍照海内，故立三公九卿以辅翼之。"一人，称君上。君子：执政者。《尚书·酒诰》："越庶伯君子。"传："众伯君子长官大夫统庶士有正者。"服：佩服。也指制服、征服。《论语·为政》：哀公问曰："'何为则民服？'孔子对曰：'举直错诸枉，则民服；举枉错诸直，则民不服。'"《孟子·公孙丑上》："以力服人者，非心服也，力不瞻也。"埶（shì）：权势。通"势"。《荀子·正名》："不治观者之耳目，不赂贵者之权埶。"《荀子·议兵》："临武君曰：'不然，兵之所贵者埶利也'。"埶利，形势便利。

【译文】

聪明的执政者，就是善使百姓心服。百姓心服，他就有权有势；百姓不心服，他就会丧失权势。

川渊深而鱼鳖归之

Deep water invites fishes and turtles.

川渊深而鱼鳖归之，山林茂而禽
兽归之，刑政平而百姓归之，礼仪备
而君子归之。

《荀子·致士》

Deep water invites fishes and turtles; thick woods attract birds and animals; justice and fair ruling appeal to people; established social institutions and etiquettes are magnets for gentlemen.

【注释】

荀子曰："故礼及身而行修，义及国而政明。"又曰："川渊枯则龙鱼去之，山林险则鸟兽去之，国家失政，则士民去之。"**川渊**：深水。川，河流。《尚书·禹贡》："奠高山大川。"渊，深水潭。《诗经·小雅·小旻》："战战兢兢，如临深渊，如履薄冰。"又《大雅·旱麓》："鸢飞戾天，鱼跃于渊。"**刑政**：刑罚与政令。《荀子·王制》："刑政平，百姓和。"平：公正。**礼仪**：行礼的仪式。《诗经·小雅·楚茨》："献酬交错，礼仪卒度。"**归**：向往，归附。《诗经·大雅·泂酌》："岂弟君子，民之攸归。"《管子·霸形》："近者示之以忠信，远者示之以礼义，行之数年，而民归之如流水。"

【译文】

河渊水深鱼鳖向往，山林茂密禽兽向往，刑罚和政令公平，百姓就会愿意归附，礼仪完备，君子就会向往。

道存则国存，道亡而国亡

Tao lives and the country exists. Tao dies and the country disappears.

道存则国存，道亡而国亡。

《荀子·君道》

Tao lives and the country exists. Tao dies and the country disappears.

【注释】

荀子说："道是什么？道是君主所施行的统治之术。"道：本义指道路。《易·履》："履道坦坦。"《论语·阳货》："道听途说。"引申为政治路线。《尚书·洪范》："无有作好，遵王之道；无有作恶，遵王之路。无偏无党，王道荡荡，无党无偏，王道平平，无反无侧，王道正直。"《论语·学而》："礼之用，和为贵，先王之道，斯为美。"《荀子·儒效》："道者，非天之道，非地之道，人之道也，君子所道也。"《易·系辞上》："易之为书也，广大悉备。有天道焉，有人道焉，有地道焉。"《易·说卦》："昔者圣人之作易也，将以顺性命之理。是以立天之道曰阴与阳，立地之道曰柔与刚，立人之道曰仁与义。"《荀子·君道》里说"道者，君之道也"，这与《儒效》篇中说的"道者，人之道也"同义，都是讲人道，人道指关于人事、人伦、处世的法则。

【译文】

道存国兴，道亡国灭。

道虽迩，不行不至

Near as a destination is, one cannot reach it without the exertion of traveling.

荀子说

道虽迩，不行不至；事虽小，不
为不成。其为人也多暇日者，其出人
不远矣。

《荀子·修身》

Near as a destination is, one cannot reach it without the
exertion of traveling; trivial as a thing is, one cannot com-
plete it without trying. Those who waste all their days cannot
distinguish themselves.

【注释】

荀子曰："頙步而不休，跛鳖千里；累土而不辍，丘山崇成。"老子曰："合抱之木，生于毫末；九层之台，起于累土；千里之行，始于足下。"（《老子》第64章）迩（ěr）：近。《诗经·周南·汝坟》："虽则如毁，父母孔迩。"注："迩，近也。"暇（xiá）：空闲。《诗经·小雅·何草不黄》："哀代征夫，朝夕不暇。"也指无事之时。《国语·楚语上》："官僚之暇，于是乎临之。"暇日，休息闲暇的时间。《孟子·梁惠王上》："壮者以暇日，修其孝悌忠信。"引申为闲散，怠惰，无所事事。出人：超出众人。

【译文】

道路虽然很近，如果不走就永远不能到达；事情虽然不大，如果不去做就不能成功。那种天天闲着无事的人，不可能出人头地。

道者，非天之道，非地之道，人
之道也

The Tao of the sage kings is neither the Tao of
Heaven nor the Tao of Earth.

荀子说

道者，非天之道，非地之道，人之道也，君子之所道也。

《荀子·儒效》

The Tao of the sage kings is neither the Tao of Heaven nor the Tao of Earth. Rather, it is the Tao of people, by which gentlemen should abide.

【注释】

荀子认为先王之道是人道的最高准则，它是遵循着适中（中庸）的路线而前进的。所谓适中的就是礼义。又说："事行失中，谓之奸事；知说失中，谓之奸道。奸事、奸道，治世之所弃，而乱世之所以服也。"道（dào）：规律。《易·说卦》："是以立天之道曰阴与阳，立地之道曰柔与刚，立人之道曰仁与义。"《荀子·天论》："天有常道矣，地有常数矣。"古人认为天道是支配人类命运的天神意志。《尚书·汤诰》："天道福善祸淫，降灾于夏。"人道指人类社会的道德规范。《易·系辞下》："有天道焉，有人道焉。"人道的最高准则是"先王之道"。

【译文】

先王之道不是指天之道，也不是指地之道，而是指人之道，这是君子所遵循的道。

德必称位，位必称禄

One should possess virtues proportional to one's position. One's position must be deserving of its payment.

德必称位，位必称禄，禄必称用。

《荀子·富国》

One should possess virtues proportional to one's position. One's position must be deserving of its payment. One's payment must be in accordance with the functions of one's position.

【注释】

荀子曰："量地而立国，计利而富民，度人力而授事。使民必胜事，事必出利，利足以生民。"所以说："朝无幸位，民无幸生。"**德必称位**：品德一定要和职位相称。德，道德。《易·乾·文言》："君子进德修业。"称（chèn），相当，符合。位，爵次，位次。《孟子·万章下》："天子一位，公一位，侯一位，伯一位，子男同一位，凡五等。"**禄**：俸禄，官吏的俸给。《左传·僖公二十四年》："介子推不言禄，禄亦不及。"《礼记·王制》："位定，然后禄之。"注："与之以常食。"**用**：功用，作用。《论语·学而》："礼之用，和为贵。"

【译文】

（人的）品德一定要和所处职位相称，职位一定要和俸禄相称，俸禄一定要和功用相称。

德厚者进而佞说者止

（Good governance should guarantee that）those with virtue are promoted and flatterers are dismissed.

老人家说系列丛书

德厚者进而佞说者止，贪利者退而廉节者起。

《荀子·君道》

（Good governance should guarantee that）those with virtue are promoted and flatterers are dismissed；those who are after personal gain should be dismissed to allow the virtuous and honest to take office.

【注释】

荀子说："崇尚礼仪，明审法制，国家就能正常运转；尊重贤明，使用人材，人民就通晓礼义。"**德厚者进**：品德淳厚的人得以晋升。德厚，即厚德。《易·坤》："地势坤，君子以厚德载物。"进，前进，提升。《诗经·大雅·常武》："进厥虎臣，阚如虓虎。"《列子·汤问》："迴旋进退，莫不中节。"也作"引荐"。《礼记·儒行》："程功绩事，推贤而进达之。"**佞**（nìng）：奸巧谄谀，花言巧语。《论语·先进》："是故恶夫佞者。"《史记·佞幸传》："嫣善骑射，善佞。"**起**：举用，出仕。《战国策·秦策》："起樗里子于国。"注："起，犹举也。"

【译文】

（好的政治要保证）品德淳厚者得以晋升，奸巧谄谀之人被制止；贪图私利的人被罢黜，廉洁奉公的人得到举荐。

凡得胜者，必与人也

    Those who want to win a victory must depend on the people.

凡得胜者，必与人也，凡得人者，必与道也。道也者，何也？曰：礼义、辞让、忠信是也。

《荀子·强国》

Those who want to win a victory must depend on the people; those who want to win people's hearts must conform to Tao. What is Tao? Tao is righteousness, modesty, loyalty and truth.

【注释】

与（yǔ）：选用，任用。《礼记·礼远》："选贤与能，讲信修睦。"道：道分天道、地道、人道。荀子讲道，多指人道。《荀子·儒效》："道者，非天之道，非地之道，人之道也。"礼义：行礼之仪式。义同"仪"。《荀子·礼论》："先王恶其乱也，故制礼义以分之。"《周礼·春官·肆师》："凡国之大事，治其礼仪。"辞让：谦让不受，也单说辞。《尚书·大禹谟》："禹拜，稽首固辞。"忠信：忠诚守信。《论语·颜渊》："子张问崇德辨惑。子曰：主忠信，徙义，崇德也。"《礼记·大学》："是故君子有大道，必忠信以得之，骄泰以失之。"

【译文】

要想取得胜利，必须依靠人民；要得人心，必得其道。道是什么？道就是礼仪、谦让和忠诚守信。

凡奸人之所以起者

The rise of evils and vices is rooted in . . .

凡奸人之所以起者，以上之不贵义，不敬义也。夫义者，所以限禁人之为恶与奸者也。

《荀子·强国》

The rise of evils and vices is rooted in a king's disregard and disrespect for righteousness. Righteousness is what restrains people from evil and depravity.

【注释】

荀子重义，他认为"凡为天下之要，义为本，而信次之。古者，禹汤本义务信而天下治；桀纣弃义倍信而天下乱。故为人上者，必将慎礼义，务忠信，然后可。此君人者之大本也。"起：发生，兴起。《尚书·益稷》："乃歌曰：股肱喜哉，元首起哉，百工熙哉。"《荀子·天论》："一废一起，应之以贯，理贯不乱。"义：荀子持"以义制利"的观点，"义之所在，不倾于权，不顾其利"（《荀子·荣辱》）。孔子把义和不正当得利相对立，"君子喻于义，小人喻于利"（《论语·里仁》），提倡"见利思义"（《论语·宪问》）。

【译文】

凡是奸邪之人兴起（的情况），一定是因为君王不提倡义、不敬重义的关系。义就是限制人们作恶和行奸的。

凡人有所一同

People all share common traits.

荀子说

凡人有所一同：饥而欲食，寒而欲暖，劳而欲息，好利而恶害，是人之所生而有也，是无待而然者也。

《荀子·荣辱》

People all share common traits: in famine they want food; in cold they require warmth; fatigue beckons rest; self-interest is treasured and harm is abhorred. This is people's innate nature needless of instructions.

【注释】

荀子认为，就人的本性来说，可以成为尧和禹这样的圣人，也可以成为桀和盗跖这样的恶人，可以做工匠、农民和商人，就在于其行为和习惯的积累。凡：所有的，一切的。《尚书·微子》："凡有辜罪，乃罔恒获。"《庄子·达生》："凡有貌象声色者皆物也。"一同：相同。一，一样。《孟子·离娄下》："其揆一也。"《庄子·逍遥游》："能不龟手一也。"生：本性，天性。《尚书·君陈》："惟民生厚，因物有迁。"传："言人自然之性敦厚，因所见所习之物有变迁之道。"《商君书·开塞》："民之生，不知则学。"

【译文】

大凡人都有相同之处。饿了就想吃饭，冷了就想温暖，劳累了就想休息，喜欢利益而憎恶祸害，这是人生来就有的本性，是不需要别人教导就知道的。

凡用兵，攻战之本，在乎壹民

The wholehearted support of the people is essential for the command of an army in wartime.

凡用兵，攻战之本，在乎壹民。弓矢不调，则羿不能以中微；六马不和，则造父不能以致远。

《荀子·议兵》

The wholehearted support of the people is essential for the command of an army in wartime. If the bow and the arrow have not been properly adjusted, even Yi, an excellent archer, would not hit the target. If the six coach horses have not been bred well, even Zao Fu, a skillful horseman, would not be able to drive far.

【注释】

壹民：使人民一致，齐一。壹，统一，通"一"。《商君书·赏刑》："圣人之为国也，壹赏，壹刑，壹教。"羿（yì）：人名。传说是夏代有穷国君主，善射，曾夺夏太康的王位，后被其臣寒浞所杀。《论语·宪问》："羿善射。"六马：古代帝王的车驾用六马。《尚书·五子之歌》："予临兆民，懔乎若朽索之驭六马。"造父：周时之善御者。传说曾取骏马以献穆王，王赐造父以赵城，由此为赵氏。

【译文】

用兵作战的根本原则，在于使人民齐心合力。弓和箭不调整好，羿也不能射中目标；驾车的六匹马不调理好，造父也不能驾车远行。

非我而当者，吾师也

Those who justifiably criticize me are my teachers.

荀子说

非我而当者，吾师也；是我而当者，吾友也；谄谀我者，吾贼也。故君子隆师而亲友，以致恶其贼。

《荀子·修身》

Those who justifiably criticize me are my teachers; those who agree with me when I am right are my friends; those who flatter me are my enemies. Hence, gentlemen should honor their teachers, stay close to their friends, and rightfully loathe their enemies.

【注释】

非：责难。《穀梁传·宣公十五年》："私田稼不善则非吏，公田稼不善则非民。"当（dàng）：适合，恰当。《礼记·乐记》："古者，天地顺而四时当。"汉·刘向《新序·杂事》："昔者魏武子谋事而当，群臣莫能，朝而有喜色。"是：认为是正确的。《墨子·尚同上》："国君之所是，必皆是之，国君之所非，必皆非之。"谄谀：谄媚，奉承。《论语·学而》："贫而无谄，富而无骄。"隆（lóng）：尊崇。《荀子·劝学》："学之经，莫速乎好其人，隆礼次之。"恶（wù）：憎恨，讨厌。与"好"（hào）相对。《左传·隐公三年》："周郑交恶。"

【译文】

批评我批评得正确的人，是我的老师；赞成我赞成得正确的人，是我的朋友；谄媚我的人，是我的敌人。所以，君子要尊崇老师，亲近朋友，还要痛恨自己的敌人。

夫贵为天子，富有天下

To be crowned as the emperor and hold a whole country's wealth . . .

荀子说

夫贵为天子，富有天下，是人情之所同欲也；然则从人之欲，则埶不能容，物不能赡也。

《荀子·荣辱》

It is man's common desire to be crowned as the emperor and hold a whole country's wealth. However, it's impossible to satisfy everyone's desire both in terms of social hierarch and the availability of resources.

【注释】

荀子认为，先王因此制定礼仪，划定界限，社会上有了等级，使人们各行其事，各得其宜。故曰："斩而齐，枉而顺，不同而一，夫是之谓人伦。"从（zòng）：放纵。通"纵"。《礼记·曲礼上》："欲不可从。"《汉书·王吉传》："其后复放从自若。"从人之欲，放纵人的欲望。埶（shì）：权势，通"势"。《荀子·正名》："不治观者之耳目，不赂贵者之权埶。"赡：充足，丰富。《孟子·梁惠王上》："乐岁终身苦，凶年不免于死亡，此惟救死而恐不赡，奚暇治礼仪哉！"

【译文】

贵为天子，富有天下，是人人都愿意做的；然而如果一味放纵人们的欲望，这在客观上是不允许的，物资上也是不能满足的。

父有争子，不行无礼

In fathering an outspoken son, one will not breach etiquette.

父有争子，不行无礼；士有争友，不为不义。

《荀子·子道》

In fathering an outspoken son, one will not breach etiquette. By befriending one who admonishes directly, one will not commit immoral deeds.

【注释】

这是荀子引孔子的话。鲁哀公问孔子曰："子从父命，孝乎？臣从君命，贞乎？"连问三次，孔子不答，后来孔子把这事告诉了子贡。孔子反对子对父、臣对君一味顺从，而强调争子、争臣、争友对父亲、对国家、对朋友的重要意义。争（zhèng）子：能规谏父母过失的儿子。《孝经》："父有争子，则身不陷于不义。"《孔子家语·三怒》："父有争子，不陷无礼。"争（zhèng）友：能规谏过失的朋友。争，也作"诤"。直言规劝，止人之失。汉·刘向《说苑·臣术》："有能尽言于君，用则留之，不用则去之，谓之谏；用则可生，不用则死，谓之诤。"

【译文】

父亲有能规谏父母过失的儿子，就不会做出无礼之事；士人有能规谏过失的朋友，就不会做出不义之事。

公生明，偏生暗

Impartiality breeds clarity and partiality obscurity.

荀子说

公生明，偏生暗；端悫生通，诈伪生塞；诚信生神，夸诞生惑。

《荀子·不苟》

Impartiality breeds clarity and partiality obscurity; integrity leads to reason and deception isolation; credibility fosters trust and exaggeration doubt.

【注释】

荀子说："这六条原则是君子应该慎重对待的，这是禹和桀的区别所在。"**公生明**：公，正直无私。《墨子·尚贤上》："举公义，辟私怨。"生，生长，长出。《易·系辞下》："天地之大德曰生。"**偏**：不公正。《尚书·洪范》："无偏无陂。"**暗**：原作"闇"。昏昧。《荀子·君道》："主暗于上，臣诈于下，灭亡无日矣。"**端悫**（duān què）：正直，诚实。**诈**：欺骗，假装。**神**：指人的意识和精神。《荀子·天论》："天职既立，天功既成，形具而神生。"**夸诞**（kuā dàn）：夸大虚妄，语言不实。《荀子·不苟》："言己之光美，拟于尧舜，参于天地，非夸诞也。"夸，自大，炫耀。《吕氏春秋·下贤》："富有天下而不骋夸。"诞，虚妄。《国语·楚语上》："是知天咫，安知民则，是言诞也。"

【译文】

公正无私就会光明正大；偏私不公正就会昏昧不明；正直诚实，就会通达事理；欺骗，就会蔽塞；诚信，就会形神兼备；夸诞，就会虚妄不实。

古之学者为己，今之学者为人

A gentleman studies for self cultivation; a petty man studies for self aggrandizement.

古之学者为己，今之学者为人。君子之学也，以美其身；小人之学也，以为禽犊。

《荀子·劝学》

A gentleman studies for self cultivation; a petty man studies for self aggrandizement. A gentleman studies to improve himself; a petty man studies to flatter himself.

【注释】

荀子曰："君子之学也，入乎耳，箸乎心，布乎四体，形乎动静；端而言，蝡而动，一可以为法则。小人之学也，入乎耳，出乎口。口耳之间，则四寸耳，何足以美七尺之躯哉？" **古之学者为己，今之学者为人**：君子学习是为了修养自身，小人学习是为了装饰自己给人看。古、今指君子、小人。《论语·宪问》："子曰：'古之学者为己，今之学者为人。'"邢昺《论语注疏》引西汉孔安国注："为己，履而行；为人，徒能言之。" **美**：美好。特指容貌、声色、才德或品质的好。**禽犊**：馈献之物。意谓小人之学无裨于身心，但为玩好而已，故以禽犊为譬。

【译文】

君子学习是为了充实提高自己的学问道德（为己），小人学习是为了粉饰自己给别人看（为人）。君子学习是用来修整身心，小人学习是用来装饰外在。

国危，则无乐君；国安，则无忧民

  When a state is threatened, no monarch can be at ease; when a state is at peace, its citizens will be without suffering.

国危，则无乐君；国安，则无忧民。乱则国危，治则国安。

《荀子·王霸》

When a state is threatened, no monarch can be at ease; when a state is at peace, its citizens will be without suffering. Turbulence endangers a state, and proper government secures one.

【注释】

荀子说："现在的统治者急于追求享乐，而把治理国家的事放到脑后，岂不是大错特错了吗?"危：凶险，不安。《庄子·则阳》："安危相易，祸福相生。"《荀子·赋》："忠臣危殆，谗人服矣。"《韩非子·解老》："士卒尽，则军危殆。"危殆，危险。《论语·泰伯》："危邦不入，乱邦不居。"危邦，不安宁的国家。乐君（lè jūn）：快乐的君主。《诗经·小雅·常棣》："宜尔家室，乐尔妻帑。"乱：动荡不定。和"治"相反。《韩非子·难势》："抱法处势则治，背法去势则乱。"治：政治清明安定。《易·系辞下》："黄帝尧舜垂衣裳而天下治。"

【译文】

国家危殆，就没有快乐的君主；国家安宁，就没有忧愁的百姓。动荡混乱国家危殆，政治清明国家安宁。

国无礼，则不正

Without etiquette there can be no orderly country.

国无礼，则不正。礼之所以正国也，譬之犹权衡之于轻重也，犹绳墨之于曲直也，犹规矩之于方圆也。

《荀子·王霸》

Without etiquette there can be no orderly country. Etiquette to a country is like a scale to a weight, a ruler to a straight line, a compass and square to a circle and rectangle.

【注释】

礼：规定社会行为的法则、规范、仪式的总称。《论语·为政》："道之以德，齐之以礼，有耻且格。"《荀子·礼论》："先王恶其乱也，故制礼义以分之。"正：安定。郑玄《周礼》注："正，犹定也。"高诱《吕氏春秋》注："正，治也。"权衡：称量物体轻重之具。权，秤锤；衡，秤杆。《礼记·深衣》："下齐如权衡以应平。"《庄子·胠箧》："为之权衡以称之，则并与权衡而窃之。"绳墨：匠人以绳濡墨打直线的工具。《孟子·尽心下》："大匠不为拙工改废绳墨。"《荀子·儒效》："设规矩，陈绳墨，便备用，君子不如工人。"规矩：校正方形圆形之器。《礼记·经解》："规矩诚设，不可欺以方圆。"

【译文】

国家没有礼制，就不能安定。礼制之所以能安定国家，就如同秤对于轻重，绳墨对于曲直，规矩对于方圆一样。

积土成山，风雨兴焉

Pile up the earth to make a mountain, which is conducive to the formation of the wind and rain.

荀子说

积土成山，风雨兴焉；积水成渊，蛟龙生焉。积善成德，而神明自得，圣心备焉。

《荀子·劝学》

Pile up the earth to make a mountain, which is conducive to the formation of the wind and rain; accumulate water to make a deep pool, and then dragons will appear. Accumulate good deeds to become a man of virtue, and then one will naturally acquire the greatest wisdom and a sage mind.

【注释】

荀子讲积善成德。因为他主张"人性恶"，只有多积善缘才能成就功德。"无惛惛之事者，无赫赫之功"。南朝宋·释法明《答李文州难佛不见形》："积善余庆，积恶余殃。"**积土成山**：比喻积少成多，聚小成大。《荀子·儒效》："积土而为山，积水而为海。"汉·王充《论衡·状留篇》："故夫河冰结合，非一日之寒；积土成山，非斯须之作。"**兴**：兴起，发动。《礼记·乐记》："明于天地，然后能兴礼乐也。"**积善成德**：积善，多行善举。《易·坤》："积善之家，必有余庆。"

【译文】

堆土成高山，于是就能起风兴雨；聚水成深渊，蛟龙就能生长出来。多积善行培养品德，神智从容，圣人的心志就具备了。

坚甲利兵不足以为胜

Protective armors and sharp weapons alone cannot guarantee the defeat of enemy.

坚甲利兵不足以为胜，高城深池不足以为固，严令繁刑不足以为威。由其道则行，不由其道则废。

《荀子·议兵》

Protective armors and sharp weapons alone cannot guarantee the defeat of enemy; tall ramparts and deep moats alone cannot ensure a state's safety; strict decrees and harsh punishments alone cannot assert one's authority over the people. Observing the ethics and etiquette, one can govern a state; otherwise, one is doomed to failure.

【注释】

荀子认为，治国平天下应凭借"礼"，而不能凭借"坚甲利兵，高城深池和严令繁刑"。孟子则认为治国平天下要靠"仁政"。故说："得道者多助，失道者寡助。"他们都认为坚甲利兵、高城深池并非取胜之本。坚甲利兵：坚固的盔甲、锋利的兵器，比喻军力精锐。《墨子·非攻下》："于此为坚甲利兵，以往攻伐无罪之国。"高城深池不足以为固：单靠高城深池不足以保护国家的安全。《孟子·公孙丑下》："城非不高也，池非不深也，兵革非不坚利也，米粟非不多也；委而去之，是地利不如人和也。故曰：域民不以封疆之界，固国不以山谿之险，威天下不以兵革之利。"威（wēi）：以威示人。

【译文】

只靠坚甲利兵不足以克敌致胜，城高池深不足以保卫国家的安全，严令繁刑不足以威震天下。依靠礼义就能得天下，不依靠礼义就会失天下。

见善，脩然必以自存也

Seeing goodness, one should examine oneself and emulate such goodness.

见善，脩然必以自存也；见不善，愀然必以自省也。善在身，介然必以自好也；不善在身，菑然必以自恶也。

《荀子·修身》

Seeing goodness, one should examine oneself and emulate such goodness; seeing evils, one should scrutinize oneself to find whether one commits similar vices. Identifying a virtue in oneself, one should adhere to it faithfully; locating an evil in oneself, one should feel shame and grieve as if one had invited in disaster.

【注释】

荀子曰："非我而当者，吾师也；是我而当者，吾友也；谄谀我者，吾贼也。"见善：遇到善良。《论语·季氏》："见善如不及，见不善如探汤。"脩（xiū）：做戒。《国语·鲁语下》："吾冀而朝夕脩然曰：'必无废先人。'"同"修"。修为修饰，脩为干肉，本为两字。自汉隶已互相通用。后来除干肉用"脩"字表示外两字通用。存：问候，省视。《战国策·秦策》："无一介之使以存之。"注："存，劳问也。"王念孙《尔雅》注："存，察也。"愀（qiǎo）：忧惧的样子。介然：专一，坚定不移。菑（zāi）：灾害，同"灾"。《诗经·大雅·生民》："不坼不副，无菑无害。"

【译文】

遇到善良，必定严肃地反问自己；遇到邪恶，必定谨慎地检查自己。善良在身，就要坚定不移地保持；邪恶在身，就如同遭遇灾害一样痛恨自己。

君人者，爱民而安

For a monarch, love for one's people will build a stable state.

君人者，爱民而安，好士而荣；两者无一焉，而亡。

《荀子·君道》

For a monarch, love for one's people will build a stable state; closeness and kindness to learned people will lead to a prosperous state. If the monarch can do neither of the above, he will ruin his state.

【注释】

荀子曰："君者，民之原也；原清则流清，原浊则流浊。"原，通"源"。**君人**：指皇帝或国君。《商君书·慎法》："君人者不察也，非侵于诸侯，必劫于百姓。"宋·王圮《元氏邑众尊胜幢赞》："自荷吾皇覆育之恩，君人安抚之惠。"**爱**：爱护，加惠。《商君书·更法》："法者所以爱民也。"《庄子·徐无鬼》："我欲爱民而为义偃兵，其何乎？"**士**：古代称四民中学习道艺者。《谷梁传·成公元年》："古者有四民：有士民，有商民，有农民，有工民。"注："士民，学习道艺者。"**荣**：繁荣，盛多。《素问·四气调神·大论》："天地俱生，万物以荣。"《荀子·大略》："汤旱而祷曰：'……宫室荣与？妇谒盛与？何以不雨而至斯极也！'"

【译文】

国君爱护人民，国家就安泰；亲善士人，国家就繁荣；这两条都做不到，国家就会灭亡。

君人者欲安，则莫若平政爱民矣

If the monarch wants a turmoil free state, then nothing is more important than ruling with fairness and caring for the people.

荀子说

君人者欲安，则莫若平政爱民矣；欲荣，则莫若隆礼敬士矣；欲立功名，则莫若尚贤使能矣。是君人者之大节也。

《荀子·王制》

If the monarch wants a turmoil free state, then nothing is more important than ruling with fairness and caring for the people; if he wants to win honor, then nothing outweighs observing etiquette and respecting people with knowledge; if he wants to make remarkable achievements, nothing outweighs honoring those of virtue and employing the capable. Such are the priorities of a monarch.

【注释】

荀子引孔子语曰："大节是也，小节是也，上君也；大节是也，小节一出焉，一入焉，中君也；大节非也，小节虽是也，吾无观其余矣。"**君人：**指皇帝或国君。《商君书·慎法》："君人者不察也，非侵于诸侯，必劫于百姓。"**平：**公正而有序。《诗经·小雅·节南山》："赫赫师尹，不平谓何？"《荀子·荣辱》："夫是之谓至平。"**隆礼：**尊崇礼仪。《荀子·劝学》："学之经，莫速乎好其人，隆礼次之。"**尚贤使能：**尊崇贤人，任用有才能的人。**大节：**关系存亡安危的大事，重要关键。《左传·成公二年》："唯器与名，不可以假人。君子所司也。……政之大节也。"

【译文】

国君要想平安无事，没有比执政公正有序、爱护百姓更重要的。要想得到荣耀，没有比尊崇礼仪、尊敬士人更重要的。要想建立功业，没有比尊崇贤良、任用有才能的人更重要的。这是国君最重要的事。

君子隘穷而不失，劳倦而不苟

**In poverty, a gentleman will not lose his integrity;
exhausted, he will be still committed to his work.**

君子隘穷而不失，劳倦而不苟，临患难而不忘细席之言。

《荀子·大略》

In poverty, a gentleman will not lose his integrity; exhausted, he will be still committed to his work; in adversity, he will not forget the promise he has made in more fortunate days.

【注释】

荀子曰："君子立志如穷，虽天子三公问，正以是非对。"如穷，犹安穷也。意谓君子固穷，纵然是天子三公相问，也一定要按着是非回答。**隘穷**：穷困，困窘。隘（ài），困窘。《荀子·王霸》："生民则致贫隘，使民则綦劳苦。"一说隘读è，通"厄"。穷困的意思。《孟子·公孙丑上》："遗佚而不怨，厄穷而不悯。"也通。**劳倦**（láo juàn）：疲劳，疲倦。劳，疲劳。《尚书·大禹谟》："耄期倦于勤。"**不苟**：认真，不苟且。《管子·小匡》："山泽各以其时至，则民不苟。"**细席**：铺在车、床上的褥垫。细（yīn），褥垫。细席之言，谓昔日发下的誓言。即《论语·宪问》所谓"久要不忘平生之言"。

【译文】

君子安贫乐道，不失节操；即使劳倦不会苟且，面临危难也不会忘记昔日发下的誓言。

君子耻不修，不耻见污

A gentleman will be ashamed of not cultivating himself, instead of feeling humiliated by others' insults.

君子耻不修，不耻见污；耻不信，不耻不见信；耻不能，不耻不见用。

《荀子·非十二子》

A gentleman will be ashamed of not cultivating himself, instead of feeling humiliated by others' insults; he will be ashamed of not being honest, instead of being ashamed of not having the trust of others; he will be ashamed of not being capable, instead of not being employed.

【注释】

荀子认为君子能够做到自身尊贵，却不一定能使人尊重自己；能够做到自身诚信，却不一定能使人相信自己；能够做到具备任职的才能，却不一定能使人任用自己。**君子耻不修，不耻见污**：君子以不能修养自身为耻辱，而不以被人污辱为耻辱。修，修身，修养身心。修身为儒家宣扬的教育八条目之一。污，耻辱。《汉书·晁错传》："使主内亡邪辟之行，外亡骞污之名。"**耻不信，不耻不见信**：君子以不诚信为耻辱，不以不被人信任为耻辱。信：①诚实，不欺。《论语·学而》："与朋友交而不信乎？"②信赖，信任。《论语·颜渊》："足食足兵，民信之矣。"

【译文】

君子以不能修养自身为耻辱，不以被人污辱为耻辱；以自己不能诚实守信为耻辱，不以不被人信任为耻辱；以自己无能为耻辱，不以不被人任用为耻辱。

君子崇人之德，扬人之美

A gentleman will promote others' good deeds and compliment others' merits.

君子崇人之德，扬人之美，非谄谀也；正义直指，举人之过，非毁疵也。

《荀子·修身》

A gentleman will promote others' good deeds and compliment others' merits, though not as idle flattery; a gentleman will not hesitate to embrace justice and identify others' mistakes, though he does not serve to denigrate others.

【注释】

崇：尊敬，推重。《礼记·王制》："上贤以崇德，简不肖以绌恶。"谄谀：谄，奉承，献媚。《论语·学而》："贫而无谄，富而无骄。"谀，谄媚，用不实之词奉承人。《荀子·修身》："以不善先人者谓之谄。以不善和（hè）人者谓之谀。"毁疵（huǐ cī）：毁，诽谤。《论语·卫灵公》："吾之于人也，谁毁谁誉？"疵，非议。

【译文】

君子尊崇别人的德行，赞扬别人的长处，并不是谄媚；依据正义，直接指出别人的过失，并不是诽谤。

君子耳不听淫声，目不视女色

A gentleman should not listen to licentious music, or stare at attractive beauties.

荀子说

君子耳不听淫声，目不视女色，口不出恶言。此三者，君子慎之。

《荀子·乐论》

A gentleman should not listen to licentious music, stare at attractive beauties, or utter rude remarks. A gentleman should take heed of the aforementioned three aspects of behavior.

【注释】

荀子说："姚冶之容，郑卫之声，使人之心淫；绅端章甫，舞韶歌武，使人之心庄。"**淫声**：古称郑卫之音等俗乐为淫声，以别于传统的雅乐。《论语·卫灵公》："放郑声，远佞人。郑声淫，佞人殆。"后来以淫声泛指浮靡不正派的乐调乐曲。《周礼·春官·大司乐》："凡建国，禁其淫声、过声、凶声、慢声。"注："淫声，若郑卫也。"**恶（è）言**：无礼、中伤一类的话。《礼记·祭义》："是故恶言不出于口，忿言不反于身。"《后汉书·卓茂传》："举善而教，口无恶言，吏人亲爱而不忍欺之。"**慎**：谨慎小心。《尚书·益稷》："慎乃在位。"

【译文】

君子耳不听淫乱之乐，目不贪恋女色，口不说无礼的话。这三条是君子修身养性需要特别注意的。

君子居必择乡，游必就士

If a gentleman wants to settle down, he will certainly choose a good neighborhood in which to do so; if he is on a journey, he will surely stay close to men of insight and virtue.

君子居必择乡，游必就士，所以防邪僻而近中正也。

《荀子·劝学》

If a gentleman wants to settle down, he will certainly choose a good neighborhood in which to do so; if he is on a journey, he will surely stay close to men of insight and virtue. In this way, he wards off evils and wiles and embraces fairness and truth.

【注释】

荀子强调环境对人成长的影响时说："兰槐之根是为芷，其渐之滫，君子不近，庶人不服，非其质不美也，所渐者然也。"兰槐，香草。其根为芷，入药称白芷。滫（xiǔ），臭泔水。意谓香草的根受污水沾染，所以君子不接近它，老百姓也不沾它。**居必择乡**：居住必须选择乡里。择乡的标准就是要利于成长。孔子说："里仁为美。择不处仁，焉得知？"（《论语·里仁》）孔子讲究选择风俗淳美的地方居住，荀子亦此意。**士**：士子，旧称读书人。唐·杜甫《别董颋》："士子甘旨阙，不知道里寒。"荀子说"游必就士"，士指儒士、读书人。**邪僻**：乖戾不正。《礼记·乐记》："惰慢邪僻之气不设于身体。"僻，同"僻"。**中正**：正直。《管子·五辅》："其君子上中正而下诹谀，其士民贵武勇而贱得利。"

【译文】

君子居住必定选择风俗淳美的地方，出游必定就教于有识之士，这是由于君子修身养性需要防止邪僻、接近正直之士的缘故。

君子宽而不僈，廉而不刿

A gentleman has poise but will not indulge in idleness; he is impartial and fair but will not allow justice to inflict unwarranted harm upon others.

君子宽而不慢，廉而不刿，辩而不争，察而不激，寡立而不胜，坚强而不暴，柔从而不流，恭敬谨慎而容。

《荀子·不苟》

A gentleman has poise but will not indulge in idleness; he is impartial and fair but will not allow justice to inflict unwarranted harm upon others; he is eloquent but will not argue for the sake of arguing; he is observant and sophisticated but will not be cynical; he is original and independent but will not try to overshadow others; he is strong willed but not cruel; he is flexible and obedient but will not submit to ill wills; he is attentive and cautious, but at the same time composed and inspiring of awe.

【注释】

宽：舒缓，松缓。"紧"的反义。《史记·韩非传》："宽则宠名誉之人，急则用介胄之士。"慢（màn）：怠惰。一说同"慢"。怠慢。廉：棱角，锋利。《老子》："是以圣人方而不割，廉而不刿。"刿（guì）：割，刺伤。廉而不刿，指棱角虽然锋利，但不致于伤物。辩：辩论，有口才。争：决胜负。察：观察，明察。《易·系辞上》："仰以观于天文，俯以察于地理。"激：过分率直。容：容貌，仪容。

【译文】

君子舒缓而不怠惰，方正而不伤人，辩论而不争强，明察而不激切，独立而不争胜于人，坚强而不粗暴，温顺而不放荡，恭敬谨慎而有威仪。

君子能为可贵，不能使人必贵己

A gentleman has virtue and abilities worthy of appreciation, but he cannot claim others' recognition.

君子能为可贵，不能使人必贵己；能为可用，不能使人必用己。

《荀子·大略》

A gentleman has virtue worthy of appreciation, but he cannot claim others' recognition; a gentleman has the abilities required to be entrusted with a responsible position, but he cannot demand others entrust him with such.

【注释】

荀子曰："虞舜、孝己，孝而亲不爱；比干、子胥，忠而君不用；仲尼、颜渊，知而穷于世劫，迫于暴国，而无所辟之。"意思是说虞舜和孝己孝顺父母，但却得不到父母的喜爱；比干和伍子胥忠于君上，但却得不到君主的信任；孔子和颜渊聪明多智，但因生于乱世，不但不被任用，而且无所逃避。说明君子可以具有高贵品质，但却不一定会被尊敬；可以具有任职的才能，却不一定会被任用。因为这些都与当时时势的影响有关。**能为可贵**：君子修身养性，能使自己具有被人尊敬的高尚品质。**能为可用**：能使自己具有任职的才能。

【译文】

君子能具备高尚的品德，却不能勉强别人尊敬自己；能具有任职的本领，却不能勉强别人任用自己。

君子贫穷而志广，富贵而体恭

In poverty, a gentleman will not be deprived of vision and an open mind; with wealth and power, he will remain polite and courteous.

君子贫穷而志广，富贵而体恭，安燕而血气不惰，劳倦而容貌不枯；怒不过夺，喜不过予。

《荀子·修身》

In poverty, a gentleman will not be deprived of vision and an open mind; with wealth and power, he will remain polite and courteous; at ease, he will not be idle and relaxed; exhausted, he will not display weariness; seething with anger, he will not inflict undue punishment; in delight, he will not bestow undeserved rewards.

【注释】

荀子曰："君子贫穷而志广，隆仁也；富贵而体恭，杀势也；安燕而血气不惰，柬理也；劳倦而容貌不枯，好文也；怒不过夺，喜不过予，是法胜私也。"广：宽阔，广大。《诗经·周南·汉广》："汉之广矣，不可泳思。"恭：肃敬，有礼貌。安燕：舒适安逸。燕，通"晏"。枯：憔悴。过：超越，过分。《荀子·王霸》："既能治近，又务治远；既能治明，又务见幽；既能当一，又务正百；是过者也，过犹不及也。"予：给予。通"与"。《诗经·小雅·采菽》："君子来朝，何锡予之？"

【译文】

君子虽贫穷而心志宽广，虽高贵而体貌谦恭，虽安闲而精力旺盛，虽劳累而容貌不憔悴。即使恼怒也不过分惩罚，即使喜欢也不过分给予。

君子贤而能容罢，知而能容愚

Virtuous and able, a gentleman is able to tolerate the less able; intelligent, he is able to tolerate the less enlightened.

君子贤而能容罢，知而能容愚，博而能容浅，粹而能容杂，夫是之谓兼术。

《荀子·非相》

Virtuous and able, a gentleman is able to tolerate the less able; intelligent, he is able to tolerate the less enlightened; knowledgeable, he is able to tolerate the less informed; focused, he is able to tolerate the less focused. This is known as the art of tolerance.

【注释】

荀子认为君子应该能够宽容群众，依靠群众，才能成就治理天下的大事。罢(pí)：行为不端。《荀子·王霸》："无国而不有贤士，无国而不有罢士。"罢士，行为不端的人。《国语·齐语》："罢士无伍，罢女无家。"知(zhì)：同"智"。《易·蹇》："见险而能止，知矣哉。"《论语·里仁》："择不处仁，焉得知。"愚：蠢笨，无知。《诗经·大雅·抑》："人亦有言，靡哲不愚。"博：通达，多闻。《荀子·修身》："多闻曰博，少闻曰浅。"粹：纯粹，专一。《易·乾》："刚健中正，纯粹精也。"杂：杂乱，不纯。兼：同时具有若干方面。《易·系辞下》："兼三才而两之。"

【译文】

君子贤达而能宽容不贤的人，聪明而能宽容愚笨的人，见多识广而能宽容孤陋寡闻的人，纯粹而能宽容不纯的人，这就是君子应该具有的兼容之术。

君子行不贵苟难，说不贵苟察

Even if an unseemly action requires skill and ability, gentlemen will not value it; even if an indecorous doctrine contains insight, gentlemen will not appreciate it.

君子行不贵苟难，说不贵苟察，名不贵苟传，唯其当之为贵。

《荀子·不苟》

Even if an unseemly action requires skill and ability, gentlemen will not value it; even if an indecorous doctrine contains insight, gentlemen will not appreciate it; reputation is not gained through undeserved recognition, but established through genuine acknowledgement.

【注释】

荀子说："盗跖出口成章，口才很好，名声如同日月那样和虞舜、夏禹一同流传无穷，然而君子却并不以他为榜样，因为他的行为不合礼仪。"苟：随便，虚假。《论语·子路》："君子于其言，无所苟而已矣。"《礼记·曲礼》："不苟訾，不苟笑。"郑玄《仪礼》注："苟，假也。"当（dàng）：适合，恰当，真实。《礼记·乐记》："古者，天地顺而四时当。"汉·刘向《新序·杂事》："昔者魏武子谋事而当，群臣莫能，朝而有喜色。"高诱《吕氏春秋》注："当，犹实也。"

【译文】

君子的行为，不以虚假的难能为可贵；学说，不以虚假的明察为可贵；名声，不以虚假的流传为可贵，只以其真实为可贵。

君子养心，莫善于诚

As to a gentleman's self cultivation, nothing outweighs his sincerity and truthfulness.

君子养心，莫善于诚。致诚，则无它事矣，唯仁之为守，唯义之为行。

《荀子·不苟》

As to a gentleman's self cultivation, nothing outweighs his sincerity and truthfulness. Apart from that, he has no other concerns but to remain benevolent and behave in accordance with morality and justice.

【注释】

荀子曰："夫诚者，君子之所守也，而政事之本也；唯所居，以其类至；操之则得之，舍之则失之。"真诚是君子必须执守的，是治政的基础。**诚**：真诚，真实。《易·乾》："修辞立其诚，所以居业也。"**致**：尽，极。《荀子·荣辱》："志意致修，德意致厚，智虑致明，是天子之所以取天下也。"郑玄《礼记》注："致，行之至也。"**守**：保持，主持。《易·系辞下》："圣人之大宝曰位，何以守位曰仁。"《荀子·王霸》："有以守多，能无狂乎?"注："守多，谓自主百事者也。"**行**：实行。《论语·先进》："冉有问：'闻斯行诸?'子曰：'闻斯行之。'"

【译文】

君子修养身心，没有比真诚更好的了。做到真诚，就基本上没有什么可做的了，只要用仁守身、用义行事就可以了。

君子役物，小人役于物

A gentleman makes use of worldly objects, while a petty man is burdened by them.

君子役物，小人役于物。

《荀子·修身》

A gentleman makes use of worldly objects, while a petty man is burdened by them.

【注释】

这是荀子引用古书中的话。意即说明"志意修，则骄富贵；道义重，则轻王公。内省而外物轻"的道理。孟子说："饱乎仁义也，所以不愿人之膏粱之味也；令闻广誉施于身，所以不愿人之文绣也。"**役物**：役使外物，使物为我所用。《荀子·正名》："故无万物之美而可以养乐，……夫是之谓重己役物。"《汉书·刑法志》："夫人……爪牙不足以供耆欲，趋走不足以避利害，无毛羽以御寒暑，必将役物以为养，任智而不恃力。"**役于物**：为外物所役使。

【译文】

君子役使外物，小人为外物所役使。

君子易知而难狎

A gentleman is approachable but not easy to behave towards in an indecorously familiar way.

君子易知而难狎，易惧而难胁；畏患而不避义死，欲利而不为所非；交亲而不比。

《荀子·不苟》

A gentleman is approachable but not easy to behave towards in an indecorously familiar way; a gentleman is vulnerable to fear but will not be threatened; a gentleman dreads adversity but will be fearless in dying for a just cause; a gentleman seeks profit but will not pursue it by dishonorable means; a gentleman socializes with others, but not for the purpose of conspiracy.

【注释】

荀子曰："君子能亦好，不能亦好；小人能亦丑，不能亦丑。"狎（xiá）：亲近，亲密。患：灾祸，忧患。《荀子·富国》："使百姓无冻馁之患，则是圣君贤相之事也。"比：勾结。《论语·为政》："君子周而不比，小人比而不周。"

【译文】

君子容易交往，而不容易轻慢；容易恐惧，而不受胁迫；害怕灾祸却不会躲避为正义而死；希求利益却不会做不义之事；同人交往，亲近而不相互勾结。

力不若牛，走不若马

（Man's）strength cannot match that of the ox and a man cannot outrun a horse.

力不若牛，走不若马，而牛马为用，何也？曰：人能群，彼不能群也。

《荀子·王制》

（Man's）strength cannot match that of the ox and a man cannot outrun a horse. However, oxen and horses are reigned by people. What lies behind that? The reason is that people constitute an organized society while the oxen and horse do not.

【注释】

荀子曰："人何以能群？曰：分。分何以能行？曰：义。故义以分则和，和则一，一则多力，多力则强，强则胜物。故宫室可得而居也。故序四时，裁万物，兼利天下，无它故焉，得之分义也。故人生不能无群。群而无分则争，争则乱，乱则离，离则弱，弱则不能胜物。"走：疾趋，跑。《诗经·大雅·绵》："古公亶父，来朝走马。率西水浒，至于岐下。"《左传·昭公七年》："三命而俯，循墙而走。"注："言不敢安行。"群：合群。《荀子·非十二子》："一统类而群天下之英杰。"注："群，会合也。"又曰："古之所谓士仕者，厚敦者也，合群者也。"

【译文】

（人）力气不如牛大，奔跑不如马快，可是牛和马都为人所役使，这是为什么？因为人能够合群，它们不能合群。

良农不为水旱不耕

A good peasant will not lay farming aside because of flood or drought.

荀子说

良农不为水旱不耕，良贾不为折阅不市，士君子不为贫穷怠乎道。

《荀子·修身》

A good peasant will not lay farming aside because of flood or drought. A good merchant will not suspend business because of losses. A man of ambition and knowledge will not abandon his principles because of poverty.

【注释】

荀子说："身劳而心安，为之；利少而义多，为之。事乱君而通，不如事穷君而顺焉。" **良**：善良，好。《诗经·陈风·墓门》："夫也不良，国人知之。" **贾**（gǔ）：商人，指坐商。《左传·宣公十二年》："商农工贾，不败其业。" **折阅**：减低售价。阅，卖。后多称财物亏损为折阅。**士君子**：旧指有志操和学问的人。唐·韩愈《讳辩》："士君子言语行事，宜何所法守也。" **怠**：松懈，懒惰。《尚书·大禹谟》："无怠无荒，四夷来王。"《商君书·弱民》："民畏死，事乱而战，故兵农怠而国弱。"

【译文】

好的农民不会因旱涝灾害而不种庄稼，好的商人不会因为赔本而不做生意，有操守的士人不会因为贫穷而放弃道义。

流丸止于瓯臾，流言止于知者

A rolling pellet stops in a depression; a rumor will be dispelled by a wise person.

流丸止于瓯臾，流言止于知者。

《荀子·大略》

A rolling pellet stops in a depression; a rumor will be dispelled by a wise person.

【注释】

这是荀子引用的俗语，并说："此家言、邪学之所以恶儒者也。是非疑则度之以远事，验之以近物，考之以平心，流言止焉，恶言死焉。"**流丸**：滚动的圆球。**瓯臾**：瓦器。喻地势低洼不平。瓯（ōu），盆盂类瓦器。《淮南子·说林》："狗彘不择瓯瓯而食。"**流言**：带有诽谤性的话。《礼记·儒行》："久不相见，闻流言不信。"

【译文】

滚动的泥丸会在低洼之处停住，流言蜚语会在明智者那里止住。

马骇舆，则君子不安舆

If the carriage horses are frightened, gentlemen in the carriage cannot ride safely.

马骇舆，则君子不安舆；庶人骇政，则君子不安位。马骇舆，则莫若静之；庶人骇政，则莫若惠之。

《荀子·王制》

If the carriage horses are frightened, gentlemen in the carriage cannot ride safely; if the subjects are appalled by the governance, the monarch will not be able to keep a stable state under his rule. It is best to calm frightened horses down, and to soothe appalled subjects with benevolent policies.

【注释】

骇（hài）：马受惊。《左传·哀公二十三年》："知伯视齐师，马骇，遂驱之。"舆（yú）：车。庶人：平民百姓。《论语·季氏》："天下有道，则庶人不议。"静：安静。《墨子·非攻》："神民不违，天下乃静。"静之，使安静。惠：仁爱，宽厚。《尚书·皋陶谟》："安民则惠，黎民怀之。"传："惠，爱也。"

【译文】

驾车的马受到惊吓，君子在车上就不能安稳；百姓受到政治惊吓，执政者就不能安泰。马受惊，最好的办法是使它安静下来；百姓受惊，最好的办法是实施仁政。

明主尚贤能而飨其盛

A wise monarch respects the noble and entrusts the able, and hence can share their achievements.

荀子说

明主尚贤能而飨其盛，暗主妒贤畏能而灭其功。

《荀子·臣道》

A wise monarch respects the noble and entrusts the able, and hence can share their achievements; an ill-judged monarch envies the noble and doubts the able, and consequently ignores their feats of achievement.

【注释】

荀子曰："明主好同，而暗主好独。"**明主**：贤圣之君主。也尊称曰"明上"、"明王"。《晏子春秋·问下》："命之曰狂僻之民，明上之所禁也。"《尚书·说命中》："明王奉若天道，建邦设都。"**尚贤能**：尚贤使能。尚，尊崇。《论语·阳货》："君子尚勇乎？"尚贤，尊崇贤人。《易·大畜》："刚上而尚贤。"能，才能。《尚书·大禹谟》："汝惟不矜，天下莫与汝争能。"《周礼·天官·大宰》："以八统诏王驭万民：一曰亲亲，二曰敬故，三曰进贤，四曰使能。"**飨**（xiǎng）：享有，享受。通"享"。《国语·晋语》："赖三子之功，而飨其禄位。"《汉书·沟洫志》："此渠皆可行舟，有余则用溉，百姓飨其利。"**盛**：丰盛。引申为勋业。**妒**：嫉妒。**灭**：淹没。《易·大过》："过涉灭顶。"

【译文】

英明之主尊贤使能，因而能够享受大臣们的丰功伟绩；昏庸之君嫉贤妒能，因而埋没了大臣们的功绩。

明主有私人以金石宝玉

A wise monarch may bestow gold and jewelry in private . . .

荀子说

明主有私人以金石宝玉，无私人以官职事业。

《荀子·君道》

A wise monarch may bestow gold and jewelry in private but will not confer office without proper cause.

【注释】

荀子认为执政者私自送人官职，对双方都是有害的。"彼不能而主使之，则是主暗也；臣不能而诬能，则是臣诈也。主暗于上，臣诈于下，灭亡无日。俱害之道也。"他以周文王举用太公为例，指出：周文王不是没有亲戚、子弟，但他却在渔人中举用太公治理天下，言听计从，把大权交给他。而他的亲戚子弟却当上了大夫诸侯，享受荣华富贵。这正是"举天下之大道，立天下之大功，然后隐其所怜所爱，其下犹足以为天下之显诸侯"。私：私自，私下。《左传·宣公十六年》："晋侯使士会平王室，定王享之，原襄公相礼，殽烝，武子私问其故。"武子，士会之谥。《论语·为政》："吾与回言终日，不违，如愚。退而省其私，亦足以发，回也不愚。"回，颜渊。

【译文】

英明的君主有把金石宝玉私下送人的，没有把官职事业私下送人的。

木受绳则直，金就砺则利

A timber can be made straight using the ink mark left by an unbent line; metal instruments can be made sharp through whetting.

荀子说

木受绳则直，金就砺则利，君子
博学而日参省乎己，则知明而行无
过矣。

《荀子·劝学》

A timber can be made straight using the ink mark left by an unbent line; metal instruments can be made sharp through whetting. Similarly, a gentleman who is erudite and examines himself daily will be wise in both thought and action.

【注释】

荀子认为，"木直中绳，輮以为轮，其曲中规，虽有槁暴，不复挺者，輮使之然也"。輮（róu），同"揉"。**绳**：木工用以画直线的工具。即墨线。《尚书·说命上》："惟木从绳则正，后从谏则圣。"《庄子·马蹄》："匠人曰：我善治木，曲者中钩，直者应绳。"**金就砺则利**：金属之器经过磨石磨治就会变得锋利。金，称戈矛之属。砺：磨治。《尚书·费誓》："砺乃锋刃，无敢不善。"

【译文】

木材经木匠用墨线比量就可以取直；金属之器经磨石打磨就能锋利；君子广博地学习，再每日省察自身，就会聪明智慧，行动不犯错误。

目不能两视而明，耳不能两听而聪

Eyes do not see clearly when trying to focus on two points; ears do not hear clearly if tuned to two sounds.

目不能两视而明，耳不能两听而聪。螣蛇无足而飞，梧鼠五技而穷。

《荀子·劝学》

Eyes do not see clearly when trying to focus on two points; ears do not hear clearly if tuned to two sounds. The flying serpent has no limbs and yet it can soar; the flying squirrel has five abilities but is not focused so that it cannot use any to success when it finds itself in extreme circumstances.

【注释】

荀子强调专一。故曰："行衢道者不至，事两君者不容。"螣（téng）蛇：传说中的神蛇。郭璞注："龙头，能兴云雾而游其中也。"梧鼠：原作鼫（shí）鼠。亦称石鼠、土鼠。《尔雅·释兽》中"鼫鼠"注："形大如鼠，头似兔，尾有毛，青黄色，好在田中食粟豆，关西呼为鼱鼠。"五技而穷：谓梧（鼫）鼠能飞而不能上屋，能缘而不能穷木，能游而不能度谷，能穴而不能掩身，能走而不能先人。后因以梧鼠之技喻技能虽多而不精。

【译文】

眼睛不能同时看清楚两处，耳朵不能同时听清楚两种声音。螣蛇没有脚却能飞上天，鼫鼠虽有五种技能却（因用心不专而）受到困窘。

能当一人，而天下取

If a worthy person is appointed to office, the state will be ruled properly.

能当一人，而天下取；失当一人，而社稷危。

《荀子·王霸》

If a worthy person is appointed to office, the state will be ruled properly; if an unworthy person is appointed, the state will fall.

【注释】

荀子列举汤用伊尹、文王起用太公、武王起用召公、成王起用周公的例子，特别说："齐桓公闺门之内，县乐、奢泰、游玩之脩，于天下不见谓脩，然九合诸侯，一匡天下，为五伯长。是亦无它故焉，知一政于管仲也。"并说："能当一人，则身有何劳而为？垂衣裳而天下定。"这是"君人者之要守也"。当（dàng）：适当，恰当。《礼记·乐记》："古者，天地顺而四时当。"取：治理。《老子》第5章："以正治国，以奇用兵，以无事取天下。"失当：不得当。马王堆汉墓帛书《经法·国次》："变故乱常，擅制更爽，心欲是行，身危有殃，是谓过极失当。"

【译文】

能起用一个恰当的人，国家就能得到治理；起用一个不恰当的人，国家就会面临危亡。

蓬生麻中，不扶而直

If fleabane grows up in the midst of straight hemp, it will stand erect without support.

老人家说系列丛书 荀子说

蓬生麻中，不扶而直；白沙在涅，与之俱黑。

《荀子·劝学》

If fleabane grows up in the midst of straight hemp, it will stand erect without support. If white sand is mixed with mud, it too will turn black.

【注释】

荀子强调后天教育和生存环境对人的影响是起决定作用的。他说："不同国度的孩子，初生下来，他们的哭声是相同的，长大以后，他们的习俗差别很大，这是由于后天教化而使他们发生了改变。"**蓬生麻中：**蓬草生长在挺直的麻杆当中，不扶自直。比喻良好的环境对人成长的影响。《颜氏家训·风操》："昔在江南，目能视而见之，耳能听而闻之，蓬生麻中，不劳翰墨。"蓬，草名，蓬蒿。《诗经·召南·驺虞》："彼茁者蓬。"麻，指麻类植物。杆高而直，皮韧，沤之可织布。雄麻质佳，雌麻粗硬不洁白，用以作丧服用。**涅：**《说文》："涅，黑土在水中也。"

【译文】

蓬蒿生长在笔直的麻类植物中间，不用绑扶就能长得很直；把白沙和黑土放在一起，白沙也会被染黑。

强本而节用，则天不能贫

Encourage farming and frugality, and Heaven will spare people from poverty.

强本而节用，则天不能贫；养备而动时，则天不能病；循道而不贰，则天不能祸。

《荀子·天论》

Encourage farming and frugality, and Heaven will spare people from poverty. Accumulate sufficient resources and farm in good time, and Heaven will not bring suffering upon people. Conform to the Tao faithfully, and Heaven will not allow disaster and catastrophe to befall people.

【注释】

荀子进一步说："水旱不能使之饥，寒暑不能使之疾，妖怪不能使之凶。本荒而用侈，则天不能使之富；养略而动罕，则天不能使之全；倍道而妄行，则天不能使之吉。"本：古籍中常以本指农桑，以末指工商。《史记·文帝纪》十三年："农，天下之本，务莫大焉。"本务指农桑。备：富足。《荀子·礼论》："故虽备家，必逾日然后能殡。"动：劳作。《孟子·滕文公上》："使民盼盼然将终岁勤动，不得以养其父母。"病：苦，困。《广雅·释诂》："病，苦也。"《左传·襄公二十四年》："范宣子为政，诸侯之币重，郑人病之。"循：依照，顺着。不贰：专一，无二心。

【译文】

加强农桑，励行节约，天就不会使人贫穷；养料充足，不误农时，天就不会使人困苦；顺行天道，专一不二，天就不会使人遭受灾祸。

轻田野之税，平关市之征

Lower the agriculture tax, and exempt the trading tax.

轻田野之税，平关市之征，省商贾之数，罕兴力役，无夺农时，如是则国富矣。

《荀子·富国》

Lower the agriculture tax, exempt the trading tax, restrain the proportion of businessmen in society, and recruit fewer peasants to do manual work so that they will not miss the seasons for farming. Doing such will make a prosperous country.

【注释】

荀子主张免除关市之征，孟子也说过"昔者文王之治岐也，耕者九一，仕者世禄，关市讥而不征"（《孟子·梁惠王下》）。**轻**：分量小，与"重"相对。《尚书·吕刑》："上刑适轻下服，下刑适重上服，轻重诸罚有权。"《孟子·梁惠王上》："权，然后知轻重，度，然后知长短。"减少分量也说轻。**平关市之征**：免除关市的税收。平，除。关市，人员物资聚集之地。《逸周书·大聚》："关市平，商贾归之。"《周礼·天官·大宰》："七曰关市之赋。"疏："王畿四面皆有关门，及王之市廛二处。"**省**（shěng）：减省，减少。《左传·僖公二十一年》："贬食省用，务穑劝分。"**力役**：征用民力。《汉书·五行志》："是时民患上力役解于公田。"

【译文】

减轻农业税，免除集市的税收，减少从商人员（而增加农业人口），少征用民力，使农民耕种不误时令，这样国家就能富足。

人生而有欲

Men are born with desires.

人生而有欲，欲而不得，则不能无求；求而无度量分界，则不能无争；争则乱，乱则穷。

《荀子·礼论》

Men are born with desires. If their desires haven't been satisfied, they won't stop pursuing them. If the pursuit goes beyond normal limits, disputes will arise. Disputes usher in turbulence and turbulence begets trouble and disaster.

【注释】

欲：贪欲。欲分物欲、情欲、色欲。《礼记·礼运》："何谓人情？喜、怒、哀、惧、爱、恶、欲。"求：寻求，探索。《诗经·小雅·伐木》："嘤其鸣矣，求其友声。"《孟子·告子上》："求则得之，舍则失之。"荀子说的"求"有强求的意思。度量：测量长短多少的器具。分界：界限。争：争夺，决胜负。乱：动荡不定。与"治"相反。《韩非子·难势》："抱法处势则治，背法去势则乱。"穷：困厄。《论语·卫灵公》："君子亦有穷乎？"

【译文】

人生下来就有贪欲之心，欲望得不到满足就不能停止求取；求取如果没有限度，就不能不去争夺；争夺就会使社会动荡不定，动荡不定就会发生困厄。

人无法则怅怅然

Without laws and rules, people will behave arrogantly.

人无法则伥伥然；有法而无志其义则渠渠然；依乎法而又深其类，然后温温然。

《荀子·修身》

Without laws and rules, people will behave arrogantly. Not understanding laws and rules, people will feel uneasy. Observing laws and rules and possessing a thorough understanding of them makes for a composed person.

【注释】

荀子曰："好法而行，士也；笃志而体，君子也；齐明而不竭，圣人也。"**伥伥**(chāngchāng)：伥，狂也。今作"猖"。《礼记·仲尼燕居》："治国而无礼，譬犹瞽之无相与，伥伥乎其何之。"**志**：记识事物。通"识"。《庄子·逍遥游》："《齐谐》者，志怪者也。"**渠渠**(jùjù)：局促不安貌。**类**：种类。《易·乾》："本乎天者亲上，本乎地者亲下，则各从其类也。"又《系辞上》："方以类聚，物以群分。"**温温**：柔和貌。《诗经·小雅·宾之初筵》："宾之初筵，温温其恭。"笺："温温，柔和也。"

【译文】

人没有法度制约行为就会狂妄；有法度但不识其义，就会局促不安；依法行事而又深明法理，才会泰然自若。

人无礼，则不生

Those who ignore etiquette will not survive.

人无礼，则不生；事无礼，则不成；国家无礼，则不宁。

《荀子·修身》

Those who ignore etiquette will not survive. An action neglecting etiquette will not end in success. A nation which casts etiquette aside will not maintain stability in its society.

【注释】

荀子认为"礼"可以使社会上每个人的贵贱、长幼、贫富都有恰当的等级地位，"礼"是人所以生存、事情所以成功、国家所以安宁的保证。**人无礼，则不生**：孔子说："不学礼，无以立。"（《论语·季氏》）与此同义。礼，孔子及儒家的政治与伦理范畴。孔子主张"以礼让为国"（《论语·里仁》），提出"非礼勿视，非礼勿听，非礼勿言，非礼勿动"（《论语·颜渊》），孟子将仁、义、礼、智作为基本的道德范畴，说"辞让之心，礼之端也"（《孟子·公孙丑上》），视礼为人的首要德行。荀子更加重视"礼"，说"礼者，贵贱有等，长幼有差，贫富轻重皆有称者也"（《荀子·富国》）。

【译文】

为人不讲礼仪，就不能生存；做事不讲礼仪，就不能成功；国家不讲礼仪，就不得安宁。

人之情，食欲有刍豢

It is common for people to want to have meat for food.

人之情，食欲有刍豢，衣欲有文绣，行欲有舆马，又欲夫余财蓄积之富也，然而穷年累世不知足，是人之情也。

《荀子·荣辱》

It is common for people to want to have meat for food, to have finery for attire, to have carriages for travel and to have wealth accumulated. However, although time advances, people's desires always remain unsatisfied, which is due to human nature.

【注释】

荀子认为人一生下来，本来就是小人，不经过老师教诲，不经过学习，就只能看到财利、只知道吃喝而已。**情**：感情，情绪。《荀子·正名》："性之好、恶、喜、怒、哀、乐谓之情。"引申为事物的本性。**刍豢**（chú huàn）：牛羊犬豕之类的家畜。《孟子·告子上》："故理义之悦我心，犹刍豢之悦我口。"南宋朱熹《孟子集注》："草食曰刍，牛羊是也；谷食曰豢，犬豕是也。"**文绣**：绣有彩色花纹的纺织品或衣服。《墨子·节葬下》："文绣素练，大鞅万领。"《孟子·告子上》："令闻广誉施于身，所以不愿人之文绣也。"注："文绣，绣衣服也。"**舆**（yú）**马**：车马。《荀子·劝学》："假舆马者非利足也，而致千里。"**穷年累世**：世世代代。连接不断，时间很长。

【译文】

人吃饭想要有肉食，穿衣服想穿漂亮的，行路希望有车马，还想要有积蓄的财富，这样世世代代不知道满足，这是人的本性。

仁义德行，常安之术也

Beneficence and morality is the path to long-lasting peace.

仁义德行，常安之术也，然而未必不危也；污漫突盗，常危之术也，然而未必不安也。故君子道其常，小人道其怪。

《荀子·荣辱》

Beneficence and morality is the path to long-lasting peace. However, they cannot guarantee immunity to trouble and disaster. Despicability and theft line the path toward trouble and danger. However, they may offer temporary rewards. Such is the reason why gentlemen follow the normal path while petty men take the deviant way.

【注释】

常安：长久平安。汉·贾谊《新书·胎教》："故无常安之国，无宜治之民。"术：方法。《孟子·告子下》："教亦多术矣，予不屑之教诲者，是亦教诲之而已矣。"污漫：污秽卑鄙。《荀子·儒效》："行不免于污漫，而冀人之以己为修也。"又《强国》："人之所恶何也？曰：污漫争夺贪利是也。"突：穿掘。《左传·襄公二十五年》："宵突陈城。"注："突，穿也。"怪：怪异，罕见。

【译文】

仁义道德，是长久平安之道，然而未必不会发生危困；卑污盗窃，是走向危困之道，然而未必不会暂时得到好处。所以君子修行常道，小人修行诡道。

仁人之兵，所存者神，所过者化

The army headed by a benevolent and righteous person will make where it stays a well-governed place and influence all other places it traverses.

仁人之兵，所存者神，所过者化；若时雨之降，莫不说喜。

《荀子·议兵》

The army headed by a benevolent and righteous person will make where it stays a well-governed place and influence all other places it traverses. Therefore，it is like a timely rain that comes and is agreeable to all.

【注释】

荀子讲仁人之兵是回答陈嚣提出的"仁者爱人，义者循理，然则又何以兵为？"的问题。荀子举"尧伐驩兜，舜伐有苗，禹伐共工，汤伐有夏，文王伐崇，武王伐纣"的例子，并说："皆以仁义之兵行于天下也。故近者亲其善，远方慕其义；兵不血刃，远迩来服；德盛于此，施及四极。"**存神过化**：存止之处，神妙莫测；所过之处，受到感化。也作"过化存神。"《孟子·尽心上》："夫君子所过者化，所存者神。"《论语·学而》："夫子之求之也，其诸异乎人之求之与"南宋朱熹《集注》："圣人过化存神之妙，未易窥测。"言圣人具盛德，所经之处，人人无不被感化；心所存主之处，神妙莫测。存，存止之处。

【译文】

仁义之师，所到之处，神妙莫测；所过之处，无不受到感化；如同及时雨降落，没有不喜欢的。

荣辱之大分，安危、利害之常体

The fundamental difference between honor and disgrace lies in people's attitudes towards danger and interest.

荣辱之大分，安危、利害之常体：先义而后利者荣，先利而后义者辱；荣者常通，辱者常穷；通者常制人，穷者常制于人；是荣辱之大分也。

《荀子·荣辱》

The fundamental difference between honor and disgrace lies in people's attitudes towards danger and interest：those who put righteousness before interest are honorable and those who do otherwise are disgraceful. The honorable will flourish and the disgraceful will suffer poverty. The flourishing dominates others, while the poor are ruled by others. Such is the fundamental difference between honor and disgrace.

【注释】

大分：大体，要领。《荀子·劝学》："礼者，法之大分，类之纲纪也。"**常体**：通常的状态。常，恒久，经常。《易·系辞上》："动静有常，刚柔断矣。"体，器物的形体，形状。

【译文】

荣耀和耻辱的根本区别在于对待安危、利害的态度上：先取义而后取利者则光荣，先取利而后取义者则耻辱。荣者通达，辱者穷困。通达者统治人，穷困者被人统治，这就是荣耀和耻辱的根本区别。

入孝出弟，人之小行也

Obedience to one's parents and respecting the elders
in a society is the most basic kind of virtue.

入孝出弟，人之小行也；上顺下笃，人之中行也；从道不从君，从义不从父，人之大行也。

《荀子·子道》

Obedience to one's parents and respecting the elders in a society is the most basic kind of virtue. Showing compliance towards one's superiors and kindness to one's subordinates is the moderate kind of virtue. Following righteousness rather than one's monarch, and complying to morality rather than to one's father is the highest kind of virtue.

【注释】

入孝出弟：在家孝顺父母，出门尊敬长上。孝弟，也作"孝悌"。其实把"孝"和"弟"并称则始于孔子弟子有若，他说："其为人也孝弟，而好犯上者，鲜矣；不好犯上，而好作乱者，未之有也。君子务本，本立而道生。孝悌也者，其为仁之本与！"（《论语·学而》）小行：低等的品行。行，行为。《论语·公冶长》："今吾于人也，听其言而观其行。"上顺下笃：对上顺从，对下厚道。顺，顺从，顺应。与"逆"相对。《易·革》："小人革面，顺以从君也。"笃，笃厚，真诚。《论语·泰伯》："君子笃于亲，则民兴于仁。"中行：中等、平常的品行。大行：崇高的德行。

【译文】

在家孝顺父母，出门尊敬长辈，这是人低等的德行；对上顺从，对下厚道，这是人中等的德行；顺从仁道而不顺从君王，顺从道义而不顺从父亲，这才是人上等的德行。

善学者，尽其理

A good learner seeks a thorough understanding of knowledge.

善学者，尽其理；善行者，究其难。

《荀子·大略》

A good learner seeks a thorough understanding of knowledge; a good man of action seeks a clear understanding of the obstacles to be confronted.

【注释】

荀子说："君子对待学习就如同蝉蜕一样，反复地起着变化。"**善**：擅长，善于。《商君书·农战》："善为国者，仓廪虽满，不偷于农。"《史记·淮阴侯传》："故善用兵者不以短击长，而以长击短。"**尽其理**：完全做到符合礼节。尽，竭，完。《易·系辞上》："书不尽言，言不尽意。"引申为达于极限。《庄子·齐物论》："至矣尽矣，不可以加矣。"理，道理，法则。《易·系辞上》："易简而天下之理得矣。"《礼记·仲尼燕居》："礼也者，理也。"疏："理，谓道理，言礼者使万物合乎道理也。"**究**：穷，极。《易·说卦》："其究躁卦。"注："究，极也。"《庄子·盗跖》："穷美究势，至人之所不得逮，贤人之所不能及。"**难**（nán）：不容易。《尚书·大禹谟》："惟帝其难之。"

【译文】

善于学习的人，一定会完全弄明白事物的道理；善于实践的人，一定会完全弄明白事物的难处。

伤良曰谗，害良曰贼

Making false and malicious statements about the innocent is termed slander.

荀子说

伤良曰谗，害良曰贼。是谓是，非谓非，曰真。窃货曰盗，匿行曰诈，易言曰诞。

《荀子·修身》

　　Making false and malicious statements about the innocent is termed slander. Fabricating a false charge against the guiltless is termed chicanery. Confirming the right and acknowledging the wrong is termed truthfulness. Stealing other's possessions is termed theft. Concealing one's actions is termed deceit. Groundless boasting is termed absurd.

【注释】

　　荀子说："取舍没有一定标准，叫做无常。保利弃义，叫做大贼。"**谗**（chán）：说别人的坏话。《庄子·渔父》："好言人之恶谓之谗。"**贼**：败坏，伤害。《论语·先进》："子路使子羔为费宰，子曰：贼夫人之子。"注引包咸："子羔学未熟习而使为政，所以为贼害。"犹今说误人子弟。**真**：真实，与"假"相对。**匿**：隐藏。《尚书·盘庚上》："不匿厥指。"**诈**：欺骗，假装。**易**：轻视。《论语·学而》："贤贤易色。"**诞**：放诞，虚妄。《国语·楚语上》："是知天咫，安知民则，是言诞也。"

【译文】

　　中伤善良，叫做谗害；陷害善良，叫做贼害。是就说是，非就说非，叫做真实。偷窃财货，叫做盗贼。隐匿行动，叫做奸诈。信口开河，叫做妄诞。

赏不欲僭，刑不欲滥
No excessive rewards or punishments.

赏不欲僭，刑不欲滥。赏僭，则利及小人；刑滥，则害及君子。若不幸而过，宁僭无滥。

《荀子·致士》

No excessive rewards or punishments. Undue rewards will benefit the underserved and excessive punishments may harm the innocent. If a mistake has to occur, it is better to benefit the undeserved than to punish the innocent.

【注释】

荀子认为，赏赐过分虽然可能使小人得到好处，也比刑罚过滥伤及好人要好一些。赏：对有功者赐与财物、官爵等。《尚书·泰誓下》："功多有厚赏。"僭(jiàn)：差失，过分。《诗经·商颂·殷武》："不僭不滥，不敢怠遑。"《左传·襄公二十六年》："赏僭则惧及淫人，刑滥则惧及善人，若不幸而过，宁僭无滥。"滥：过度。《逸周书·程典》："生稼省用，不滥其度。"宁(nìng)：副词。宁愿，宁可。《尚书·大禹谟》："与其杀不辜，宁失不经。"《庄子·秋水》："宁其死为留骨而贵乎？宁其生而曳尾于涂中乎？"

【译文】

赏赐不可过分，刑罚不可过滥。赏赐过分会使小人得利；刑罚过滥会伤及好人。如不得已而发生错误，宁可使小人得利也不可伤及好人。

尚贤使能，赏有功，罚有罪

Honor the virtuous, appoint the capable, award those with achievements, and punish the guilty.

尚贤使能，赏有功，罚有罪，非独一人为之也。彼先王之道也，一人之本也，善善恶恶之应也。

《荀子·强国》

Honor the virtuous, appoint the capable, award those with achievements, and punish the guilty. These principles were not established by any single person, but are the principles handed down by ancient sage kings. Such principles can unite people and reflect the idea of rewarding the good and punishing the evil.

【注释】

尚贤：尊崇贤人。《易·大畜》："刚上而尚贤。"《墨子》有《尚贤篇》。使能：使用有才能的人。一人之本：统一人民的根本。一，统一。《韩非子·五蠹》："法莫如一而固。"唐·杜牧《阿房宫赋》："六王毕、四海一。"本，事物根基或主体。《论语·学而》："君子务本。"《商君书·定分》："法令者，民之命也，为治之本也，所以备民也。"善善恶恶：奖善嫉恶，好恶分明。应（yìng）：应和。《易·乾·文言》："同声相应，同气相求。"

【译文】

尊崇贤圣，使用有才能的人，奖赏有功的人，处罚有罪的人，这并不是哪一个人创立的，这是先王之道，是统一人民的根本原则。这是和奖善嫉恶相对应的。

少而不学，长无能也

Having not studied in youth, one will not be able to fill an office in one's maturity.

少而不学，长无能也；老而不教，死无思也；有而不施，穷无与也。

《荀子·法行》

Having not studied in youth, one will not be able to fill an office in one's maturity. Having not counseled others in one's senior years, one will not be missed after death. Having not obliged others with one's riches, one cannot expect others' help in times of poverty.

【注释】

少（shào）：年幼，年轻人，"老"的对称。《左传·襄公三十一年》："子皮欲使尹何为邑，子产曰：'少，未知可否。'"无能：没有才能，没有任职的才能。《论语·卫灵公》："君子病无能焉，不病人之不己知也。"教（jiāo）：传授。《左传·襄公三十一年》："教其不知，而恤其不足。"思：思慕，想念。《诗经·郑风·褰裳》："子惠思我，褰裳涉溱。"施：给予。《国语·吴语》："施民所欲，去民所恶。"与：援助。《战国策·秦策一》："楚攻魏，张仪谓秦王曰：不如与魏以劲之。"

【译文】

少年不学习，长大就没有任职的才能；年老不传授经验给后人，死后就没有人怀念；富有时不知道施惠于人，贫穷了就没有人周济。

身劳而心安，为之

It is worthwhile to do things that exhaust one's body but put one's conscience at ease.

身劳而心安，为之；利少而义多，为之。事乱君而通，不如事穷君而顺焉。

《荀子·修身》

It is worthwhile to do things that exhaust one's body but put one's conscience at ease; it is worthwhile to do things that are poor in profits but rich in meaning. Prosperity gained through working for a fatuous monarch is inferior to the righteousness and peace attained by working for wise monarch in times of difficulty.

【注释】

荀子曰："良农不为水旱不耕，良贾不为折阅不市，士君子不为贫穷怠乎道。"**乱君**：昏庸无道的君主。《战国策·齐策四》："斗生于乱世，事乱君，焉敢直言正谏？"斗，王斗。《韩非子·心度》："故明君有权有政，乱君亦有权有政，积而不同，其所以立异也。"**通**：畅通。《易·系辞上》："一阖一辟谓之变，往来不穷谓之通。"**穷**：困厄。《论语·卫灵公》："君子亦有穷乎？"《孟子·尽心上》："穷不失义，达不离道。"**顺**：顺理，顺序。《论语·子路》："名不正，则言不顺，言不顺，则事不成。"

【译文】

身体虽劳苦但令内心安适的事可以做，获利虽少而合道义的事可以做。事奉昏庸无道的国君，虽然官运亨通，也不如事奉处于困境的明君更顺乎天理。

神莫大于化道，福莫长于无祸

Wisdom is no more than conforming to the laws of nature; luck is no more than being trouble free.

荀子说

神莫大于化道，福莫长于无祸。

《荀子·劝学》

Wisdom is no more than conforming to the laws of nature; luck is no more than being trouble free.

【注释】

荀子强调后天教育，他说不同国度的孩子"生而同声，长而异俗，教使之然也"。并引《诗经·小雅·小明》曰："嗟尔君子，无恒安息。靖共尔位，好是正直。神之听之，介尔景福。"要人们勤奋学习不懈怠。**神**：指人的意识和精神。《荀子·天论》："天职既立，天功既成，形具而神生。"南朝梁·江淹《别赋》："造分乎而衔涕，感寂寞而伤神。"《淮南子·俶真》："神者，智之渊也。"《兵略》："知人所不知谓之神。"王冰《素问》注："神，谓神智通悟。"**化**：遵从。高诱《淮南子》注："化，从也。"《老子》第57章："我无为而民自化。"**道**：自然与社会法则或发展规律。《老子》第1章："道可道，非常道。"《韩非子·解老》："道者，万物之所然也，万理之所稽也。""道，谓自然之道也"（河上公《老子注》）。**长**（cháng）：善，优。《孟子·公孙丑上》："'敢问夫子恶乎长？'曰：'我知言，我善养吾浩然之气'。"

【译文】

聪明莫过于遵从自然规律，幸福莫过于没有灾祸。

声乐之入人也深，其化人也速

Music is powerful in influencing people, and swift in moving people.

声乐之入人也深，其化人也速，故先王谨为之文。

《荀子·乐论》

Music is powerful in influencing people, and swift in moving people. Hence, ancient wise kings have been cautious about the establishment of rites and music.

【注释】

荀子说："音乐就是娱乐，这是人类情感必不可少的表现形式。"又说："乐中平，则民和而不流；乐肃庄，则民齐而不乱。……故先王贵礼乐而贱邪音。"声乐：声和乐都是指音乐。《论语·阳货》："恶紫之夺朱也，恶郑声之乱雅乐也。"乐，音乐。五声八音的总名。《易·豫》："先王以作乐崇德。"《吕氏春秋·古乐》："昔葛天氏之乐，三人操牛尾，投足以歌八阕。"入人：深入人心。化人：感化人心。速：快，迅速。《论语·子路》："欲速则不达，见小利则大事不成。"文：礼乐制度。《论语·子罕》："文王既没，文不在兹乎？"《集注》："道之显者谓之文，盖礼乐制度之谓。"

【译文】

音乐最容易深入人心，感化人心的速度也快，所以先王谨慎地制定礼乐制度。

声无小而不闻，行无隐而不形

No matter how tiny the voice is, it is still audible;
no matter how secretive an action is, it is still perceivable.

声无小而不闻，行无隐而不形。玉在山，而草木润；渊生珠，而崖不枯。为善不积邪，安有不闻者乎？

《荀子·劝学》

No matter how tiny the voice is, it is still audible; no matter how secretive an action is, it is still perceivable. With jade buried in the mountain, the trees and plants will be nourished. With pearls deep in the water, the banks will not dry. Doing good deeds and getting rid of evil, one will be surely known to the world.

【注释】

荀子曰："昔者瓠巴鼓琴，而沈鱼出听；伯牙鼓瑟，而六马仰秣。"声无小而不闻，行无隐而不形：声音再小也能被人听见，行为再隐秘也会被人知道。形，显露，表现。《战国策·赵策》："赵王不悦，形于颜色。"润：滋润。《易·说》："风以散之，雨以润之。"本指雨露滋润草木，这里指山中有玉，而滋润山上草木。枯：枯槁，干涸。《礼记·月令》孟夏之月："行冬令，则草木蚤枯。"《荀子·致士》："川渊枯则龙鱼去之。"

【译文】

声音再小也能被人听见，行为再隐秘也会被人知道。山里藏着宝玉，山上的树木就显得润泽；深水里生有珍珠，河岸就不会干涸。只做好事，不干坏事，没有不闻名于世的。

施薪若一，火就燥也

If the firewood is spread out, then fires will start where the dry wood congregates.

施薪若一，火就燥也；平地若一，水就湿也；草木畴生，禽兽群居。物各从其类也。

《荀子·劝学》

If the firewood is spread out, then fires will start where the dry wood congregates. Water on a flat land will flow to a wet place. Dense trees and plants invite flocks of birds and animals. Such is the way of the world, that things of the same sort flock together.

【注释】

荀子说："林木繁茂，就会召来斧头砍伐；醋酸，就会召来蚋虫繁殖。"故"言有召祸也，行有召辱也"，君子慎处之。**施**：散布。《易·乾》："云行雨施，品物流行。"注："使云气流行，雨泽施布，故品类之物，流布成形。"**燥**：干燥。《易·乾》："水流湿，火就燥。"**湿**：潮湿。也指湿润。《庄子·大宗师》："泉涸，鱼相与处于陆，相呴以湿，相濡以沫。"**畴**（chóu）：同处，同类。同"俦"。《国语·齐语》："人与人相畴，家与家相畴。"**类**：种类。《易·乾》："本乎天者亲上，本乎地者亲下，则各从其类也。"又《系辞上》："方以类聚，物以群分。"

【译文】

柴草摊开，火总是先向干燥处燃烧；在平地上，水总是先向潮湿处流淌；草木丛生，鸟兽成群居住。万物都是这样同类相聚而生活的。

水火有气而无生

Water and fire have got the rhythm of breath but have no life.

水火有气而无生，草木有生而无知，禽兽有知而无义。人有气，有生，有知亦且有义，故最为天下贵也。

《荀子·王制》

Water and fire have got the rhythm of breath but have no life; plants and trees have got life but no thoughts; animals have thoughts but no etiquette. People have the rhythm of breath, life, thoughts and etiquette and hence are the most respectable and honorable creatures under Heaven.

【注释】

荀子说："天地是生养的本始，礼义是政治的本始，君子是礼义的本始。"气：气息，呼出吸入之气。《论语·乡党》："摄齐升堂，鞠躬如也，屏气似不息者。"生：生命。《孟子·告子上》："生亦我所欲，所欲有甚于生者，故不为苟得也。"知：思想意识。《商君书·更法》："有独知之虑者，必见惊于民。"《荀子·王制》："草木有生而无知，禽兽有知而无义。"注："知为性识也。"义：礼仪，容止。《周礼·春官·肆师》："凡国之大事，治其礼仪。"汉·郑玄注："古者仪但为义，今时所谓义者为谊。"

【译文】

水火有气息而没有生命，草木有生命而没有思想意识，禽兽有思想意识而没有礼仪。人有气息、有生命、有思想意识而且有礼仪，所以人是天下最尊贵的。

岁不寒，无以知松柏

If it were not for the chilly season, pines and cypresses could not exhibit their character.

岁不寒，无以知松柏；事不难，无以知君子。

《荀子·大略》

If it were not for the chilly season, pines and cypresses could not exhibit their character. If it were not for difficulties, gentlemen could not manifest their virtues.

【注释】

荀子说："君子固穷，不失其道；劳倦困厄，不苟且偷安；患难临头，不忘平生所发下的誓言。"**岁寒**：一年的寒冬。《论语·子罕》："岁寒，然后知松柏之后彫也。"因松柏岁寒不彫，故后世诗文中常以岁寒松柏比喻在逆境中能保持节操的人。唐·刘禹锡《将赴汝州途出浚下留辞李相公》诗："后来富贵已零落，岁寒松柏犹依然。"

【译文】

不到一年中最寒冷的季节，就显不出松柏耐寒的性格；不身处艰苦的逆境中，就显不出君子的节操。

天不为人之恶寒也辍冬

Heaven will not eschew winter because people loathe the cold.

天不为人之恶寒也辍冬，地不为人之恶辽远也辍广，君子不为小人之匈匈也辍行。天有常道矣，地有常数矣，君子有常体矣。

《荀子·天论》

Heaven will not eschew winter because people loathe the cold. The Earth will not forsake its vastness because people resent remoteness. Gentlemen will not stop their actions because of petty men's roaring comments. Heaven has its eternal course to follow; the Earth has its eternal structure to guard; gentlemen have their eternal decency to maintain.

【注释】

恶（wù）：憎恨，讨厌。辍（chuò）：停，终止。《论语·微子》："耰而不辍。"辽：遥远。《左传·襄公八年》："楚师辽远，粮食将尽，必将速归。"广：宽阔，广大。《诗经·周南·汉广》："汉之广矣，不可泳思。"匈匈（xiōngxiōng）：吵嚷声。行（xìng）：行为。常道：永恒不变的道（规律）。常数：永恒不变的形势。常体：永恒不变的性状，即通常的性状、常态。

【译文】

天不会因人们讨厌寒冷而中止冬季的运行，地不会因人们讨厌遥远而缩减它的广阔，君子不会因小人的吵吵嚷嚷而废止他的行为。天有永恒不变的规律，地有永恒不变的形势，君子有永恒不变的性状。

天不言，而人推高焉

Heaven does not speak, but people honor its highness.

荀子说

天不言，而人推高焉；地不言，而人推厚焉；四时不言，而百姓期焉；夫此有常以至其诚者也。

《荀子·不苟》

Heaven does not speak, but people honor its highness. The Earth does not speak, but people respect its depth. The four seasons do not talk, but people expect their revolutions over time. Their eternal passage bespeaks their innate truth.

【注释】

荀子说："天地是至大无比的，如果不真诚，就不能感化万物了。"推：举荐，尊崇。《尚书·周官》："推贤让能，庶官乃和。"《南史·任昉传》："其为士友所推如此。"期：期限。《诗经·王风·君子于役》："君子于役，不知其期。"又《小雅·南山有台》："乐只君子，万寿无期。"也指限度。《吕氏春秋·怀宠》："征敛无期，求索无厌。"诚：真实。《礼记·乐记》："著诚去伪，礼之经也。"

【译文】

天不说话，人们都认为它最高；地不说话，人们都认为它最厚；四时不说话，人们都知道它依顺序按时运行。这是由于它们永恒不变，达到了真实的境界。

天道有常：不为尧存，不为桀亡

The course of Heaven is eternal: it does not exist for the sage kings like Emperor Yao or die due to atrocious kings like Emperor Jie.

老人家说系列丛书

天道有常：不为尧存，不为桀亡。应之以治则吉，应之以乱则凶。

《荀子·天论》

The course of Heaven is eternal：it does not exist for the sage kings like Emperor Yao or die due to atrocious kings like Emperor Jie. Governance conforming to the course of Heaven brings auspiciousness，otherwise disasters will arise.

【注释】

天道：一般指天文气象等方面的自然现象和规律。与"地道"、"人道"并称。孔子说："天道敏生，人道敏政，地道敏树。"（《孔子家语·哀公问政》）《易·说卦》："昔者圣人之作易也，将以顺性命之理。是以立天之道曰阴与阳，立地之道曰柔与刚，立人之道曰仁与义。"孔子重人事，多讲人道，少讲天道。常：恒久，经常。《易·系辞上》："动静有常，刚柔断矣。"尧：传说中之古帝陶唐氏之号，是圣君的代表。桀（jié）：夏代最后一位国君名。为古时暴君之典型，与商纣并称。应（yìng）：应和。《易·乾·文言》："同声相应，同气相求。"吉：善，利。与"凶"相对。《逸周书·武顺》："礼义顺祥曰吉。"

【译文】

天道是永恒不变的，不以人的意志为转移。它不会为圣君尧而存在，也不会因暴君桀而消失。顺应天道治之则获得吉祥，乱之则遭受灾祸。

为上则不能爱下，为下则好非其上

As the superior, one cannot tend to one's subordinates if as the subordinate, one slanders one's superiors.

为上则不能爱下，为下则好非其上，是人之一必穷也。

《荀子·非相》

As the superior, one cannot tend to one's subordinates if as the subordinate, one slanders one's superiors. Such is the principal reason that leads to failure in one's career.

【注释】

荀子认为人有三种必然不能通达的原因：在上位不能爱抚下民，在下位却好诽谤上级，这是其一；当面不顺从人家，背后又侮慢人家，这是其二；知识浅薄、操行不如人，又不能尊崇仁爱之人和明智之士，这是其三。为（wéi）：作，担当。《尚书·益稷》："子欲宣力四方，汝为。"爱：爱护，加惠。《商君书·更法》："法者所以爱民也。"《庄子·徐无鬼》："我欲爱民而为义偃兵，其何乎？"非（fěi）：诽谤。通"诽"。《荀子·解蔽》："故群臣去忠而事私，百姓怨非而不用。"注："非或为诽。"穷：困厄，不通达。《论语·卫灵公》："君子亦有穷乎？"

【译文】

在上位不能爱抚下民，在下位又好诽谤上司，这是人必然不能通达的首要原因。

闻之而不见，虽博必谬

Having heard of things but not having seen them oneself, one will err even though one is well-informed.

闻之而不见，虽博必谬；见之而不知，虽识必妄；知之而不行，虽敦必困。

《荀子·儒效》

Having heard of things but not having seen them oneself, one will err even though one is well-informed. Having seen things but not having understood them, one tends to make rash judgments even though one is aware of them. Having understood things but not translating one's understanding into actions, one will fall into bewilderment even though one has a broad understanding in different fields.

【注释】

荀子曰："不闻不见则虽当，非仁也，其道百举而百陷也。"博：多闻。《荀子·修身》："多闻曰博，少闻曰浅。"谬：差错。《汉书·司马迁传》："故《易》曰：差以毫厘，谬以千里。"识（shí）：识别，知道。《诗经·大雅·皇矣》："不识不知。顺帝之则。"又《瞻卬》："如贾三倍，君子是识。"妄：狂乱，荒诞。《易·无妄》释文："无妄，无虚妄也。"敦：惇厚，笃厚。《易·临》："敦临，吉，无咎。"《老子》："敦兮其若朴，旷兮其若谷。"有把"虽敦必困"译为"虽然知识丰富，也必然有所困顿。"也通。困：艰难，窘迫。《尚书·盘庚中》："汝不忧朕心之攸困。"《礼记·中庸》："事前定，则不困。"

【译文】

道听途说而没有亲眼所见，虽多闻也必然存在错误；亲眼所见而并不明白，虽然知道也必然虚妄不实；能够知道却不能实行，虽然知多识广也必然会遭困顿。

无德不贵，无能不官

Without virtue, one cannot deserve a high status. Without abilities, one cannot secure an official position.

无德不贵，无能不官，无功不赏，无罪不罚。朝无幸位，民无幸生。

《荀子·王制》

Without virtue, one cannot deserve a high status. Without abilities, one cannot secure an official position. Without merits, one is not entitled to awards. Without guilt, one should not face penalties. In government, no position should be attained through luck. Among the civilians, no one's livelihood depends on luck.

【注释】

荀子曰："尚贤使能，而等位不遗；折愿禁悍，而刑罚不过。百姓皆晓然知夫为善于家，而取赏于朝也；为不善于幽，而蒙刑于显也。夫是之谓定论：是王者之论也。"**贵**：位尊。《易·系辞上》："卑高以陈，贵贱位矣。"**幸生**：幸，通"倖"。侥倖于苟且生存。

【译文】

没有德操不能显贵，没有才能不能做官，没有功劳不受封赏，没有罪恶不受处罚。朝中没有侥幸的职位，民间没有侥幸的生存。

物类之起，必有所始

There must be a beginning for every single occurrence.

物类之起，必有所始；荣辱之
来，必象其德。肉腐生虫，木枯生
蠹。怠慢忘身，祸灾乃作。

《荀子·劝学》

There must be a beginning for every single occurrence.
The coming of honor or disgrace must be a reflection of one's
morals. Rotting meat nurtures maggots. Decaying wood pro-
duces woodworms. Insolently disregarding self cultivation will
beget therewith disaster and misfortune.

【注释】

荀子认为物类起始，必有所因，故曰："施薪若一，火就燥也；平地若一，水就
湿也。"柴草摊开，火总是向着干燥的一边燃烧；地面平整，水总是向潮湿的一边流
淌，这是物性。**象：**高诱《淮南子》注："象，犹随也。" **肉腐生虫，木枯生蠹：**后
成语"物腐虫生"出于此。物先腐烂而后有虫生。喻祸患之来必有其内因。宋·苏
轼《范增论》："物必先腐也，而后虫生之；人必先疑也，而后谗入之。" **蠹（dù）：**
蛀虫。《商君书·脩权》："谚曰：蠹众而木折，隙大而墙坏。"《韩非子·亡征》：
"木之折也，必通蠹；墙之坏也，必通隙。"《说文》："蠹，木中虫。"

【译文】

万物的兴起，必定有个开始；荣辱的到来，必定是
由人们自己的行为招致的。肉腐烂生蛆，木枯生虫。行
为怠慢，不注意自身修养，就要招祸。

相高下，视垅肥，序五种

In terms of identifying the terrain features and the soil quality, and scheduling the planting of five main crops . . .

相高下，视垅肥，序五种，君子不如农人；通财货，相美恶，辨贵贱，君子不如贾人。

《荀子·儒效》

In terms of identifying the terrain features and the soil quality, and scheduling the planting of five main crops, gentlemen cannot match the farm hands. In the field of the circulation of capital and goods, distinguishing the quality of goods, and determining prices, gentlemen are not equal to businessmen.

【注释】

荀子曰："君子之所谓贤者，非能徧能人之所能之谓也。"又说："说话合乎理性，办事知道缓急，才是君子的长处。"相（xiàng）：视，观察。《诗经·鄘风·相鼠》："相鼠有皮，人而无仪。"《左传·隐公十一年》："量力而行之，相时而动。"垅（qiāo）：瘠薄的土地。序：季节。五种：五谷，即黍、稷、豆、麦、麻。

【译文】

观察地势高低，识别土壤肥瘠，安排五谷种植的时令，君子不如农人；使财货流通，审察货物的等级，制定货物的价格，君子不如商人。

相形不如论心；论心不如择术

Observing one's physiognomy ranks lower than assessing one's thought. Assessing one's thought is of less weight than judging one's behavior.

荀子说

相形不如论心；论心不如择术。
形不胜心，心不胜术。

《荀子·非相》

Observing one's physiognomy ranks lower than assessing one's thought. Assessing one's thought is of less weight than judging one's behavior. Thought outweighs physiognomy and behavior outweighs thought.

【注释】

荀子重行，他说："形不胜心，心不胜术。术正而心顺之，则形相虽恶而心术善，无害为君子也；形相虽善而心术恶，无害为小人也。"孔子也重行，"行"是他对弟子进行教育的主要内容之一。他说"言之必可行"（《论语·子路》），"听其言而观其行"（《公冶长》）。**相形**：相面，相看形貌善恶，以定吉凶。相，审视。《尚书·召诰》："成王在丰，欲宅洛邑，使召公先相宅。"传："相所居而卜之。"也指形貌。**论**：评论，辩论。《礼记·王制》："凡官民材，必先论之，论辩然后使之。"《吕氏春秋·应言》："人与不入之时，不可不熟论之。"注："论，辩也。"**术**：道术。郑玄《礼记》注："术，犹道也。道，犹行也。"

【译文】

相看人的形貌，不如评论人的思想；评论人的思想，不如观察其行为。形貌胜不过思想，思想胜不过行为。

心不使焉，则白黑在前而目不见

Distracted, one cannot see white or black before one's eyes.

心不使焉，则白黑在前而目不见；雷鼓在侧而耳不闻；况于蔽者乎？

《荀子·解蔽》

Distracted, one cannot see white or black before one's eyes and cannot hear drum beats in one's ears. Likewise is the blindness of those who are kept from the truth.

【注释】

解蔽：解开蒙蔽。解，解开，消散。《孟子·公孙丑上》："万乘之国行仁政，民之悦之，犹解倒悬也。"蔽，蒙蔽。《论语·阳货》："女闻六言六蔽矣乎？"疏："蔽谓蔽塞，不自见其过也。"雷鼓：敲鼓。雷，通"擂"。《乐府诗集·钜鹿公主歌辞》："官家出游雷大鼓，细乘犊车开后户。"另一说雷鼓为古乐器名。祭祀天时使用。本文中的雷鼓应是"擂鼓"，但以"雷鼓"也可通。

【译文】

心不在焉，黑白分明的东西在眼前也看不出来，擂鼓之声在耳边也听不见，又何况是被蒙蔽了的人呢？

新浴者振其衣，新沐者弹其冠

After bathing, people will shake their apparel before putting it on. After washing their hair people will beat their hat before it is donned.

新浴者振其衣，新沐者弹其冠，人之情也。其谁能以己之瀌瀌，受人之捝捝者哉？

《荀子·不苟》

After bathing, people will shake their apparel before putting it on. After washing their hair people will beat their hat before it is donned. Such actions are common to all human beings. Who is willing to have one's clear understanding contaminated by the confusions of other's?

【注释】

荀子曰："君子洁其身，而同焉者合矣；善其言，而类焉者应矣。故马鸣而马应之，牛鸣而牛应之，非知也，其势然也。"振：摇动，抖动。《诗经·豳风·七月》："六月莎鸡振羽。"屈原《渔父》："新沐者必弹冠，新浴者必振衣。"振衣，抖掉衣服上的灰尘。弹（tán）：弹击。弹冠，用手指弹去帽子上的灰尘。瀌瀌（jiàojiào）：明察。《荀子》注曰："瀌瀌，明察之貌。瀌，尽。谓穷尽明于事。"捝捝（huòhuò）：迷惑。通"惑"。

【译文】

新洗过澡的人，总要抖抖衣服再穿；新洗过头发的人，总要弹弹帽子再戴。这是人之常情。谁肯以自己的明察而接受别人的昏乱呢？

选贤良，举笃敬，兴孝弟，收孤寡

Appoint the capable and virtuous. Promote the truthful and trustworthy. Advocate obedience to one's parents and elder brothers. Take care of orphans and the widowed.

选贤良，举笃敬，兴孝弟，收孤寡，补贫穷，如是则庶人安政矣。庶人安政，然后君子安位。

《荀子·王制》

Appoint the capable and virtuous. Promote the truthful and trustworthy. Advocate obedience to one's parents and elder brothers. Take care of orphans and the widowed. Subsidize the poor. Such actions enable the civilians to be willingly ruled. With their subjection, the monarch can secure his reign.

【注释】

荀子引古书上的话说："君者，舟也；庶人者，水也；水则载舟，水则覆舟。"
选：选择。《礼记·礼运》："选贤与能，讲信修睦。"贤良：有德行的人。举笃敬：举荐忠厚之人。举，推荐，选用。《墨子·尚贤》："故古者尧举舜于服泽之阳。"笃：忠诚厚道。《论语·泰伯》："君子笃于亲，则民兴于仁。"敬：恭敬，端肃。《易·坤》："君子敬以直内，义以方外。"《论语·子路》："居处恭，执事敬，与人忠。"兴孝弟：提倡孝悌。孝弟（xiào tì）：孝顺父母，敬爱兄长。《论语·学而》："其为人也孝弟，而好犯上者，鲜矣。"弟，也作"悌"。

【译文】

选用贤良，举荐忠厚，提倡孝悌，安抚孤寡，救济贫穷，这样百姓就安于政治了。百姓安其政，执政者也就安于其位了。

学不可以已

Learning must be never concluded.

学不可以已。青取于蓝，而青于蓝；冰生于水，而寒于水。

《荀子·劝学》

Learning must be never concluded. Though blue comes from the indigo plant, it is bluer than indigo. Ice is made from water, but it is colder than the water from which it was formed.

【注释】

荀子认为学习是不能停止不前的，要不断向前发展、推陈出新，才能不断进步。已：停止。《诗经·郑风·风雨》："风雨如晦，鸡鸣不已。" **青取于蓝，而青于蓝**：青，五色之一。蓝，蓝草，可作染料。青色从蓝草中提炼出来。但颜色比蓝草更深。这句话有版本作："青，取之于蓝，而青于蓝，冰，水为之，而寒于水。"北齐刘昼《刘子崇学》："青出于蓝而胜于蓝，染使然也。"后以"青出于蓝"比喻学生在学业成就上超过老师或后人胜过前人。唐·白居易《赋赋》："赋者，古诗之流也。始草创于荀、宋，渐恢张于贾、马。冰生乎水，初变本于《典》、《坟》；青出于蓝，复增华于《风》、《雅》。"荀子虽以继承孔子学说自居，却站在"大儒"、"雅儒"的立场上批评子夏、子游、子思、孟子为"俗儒"、"贱儒"、"腐儒"。故他在《荀子》开篇《劝学》中开门见山地提出："君子曰：学不可以已。"

【译文】

学习是不能停止不前的。青色从蓝草中提炼出来，颜色却比蓝草更深；冰是水遇冷凝结而成的，可它比水更加寒凉。

学者，非必为仕

Learning is not necessarily for an official career.

学者，非必为仕；而仕者，必如学。

《荀子·大略》

Learning is not necessarily for an official career. However, government officials must devote themselves to learning.

【注释】

荀子的意思是不论做官还是不做官，都不可以停止学习。他还以子贡问孔子的话作证。子贡对孔子说："自己对学习已经厌倦了，想停止学习去做官。"孔子说："做官事奉君主不容易，怎么能停止学习呢？"**学者，非必为仕**：学习不一定是为了做官。学者，求学的人。《论语·宪问》："子曰：古之学者为己，今之学者为人。"仕，作官。《论语·公冶长》："令尹子文三仕为令尹，无喜色。"《礼记·曲礼上》："四十曰强而仕。"**如**：谋求。《尔雅》："如，谋也。"

【译文】

学习不一定是为了做官，但做官的人一定要学习。

言必当理，事必当务

Make appropriate remarks and manage affairs properly.

言必当理，事必当务，是然后君子之所长也。

《荀子·儒效》

Make appropriate remarks and manage affairs properly; such are the merits of gentlemen.

【注释】

荀子曰："相高下，视硗肥，序五种，君子不如农人；通财货，相美恶，辨贵贱，君子不如贾人；设规矩，陈绳墨，便备用，君子不如工人。""言必当理，事必当务"才是君子的长处。当理：合理。当（dàng），适合，恰当。《礼记·乐记》："古者，天地顺而四时当。"理，道理，法则。《易·系辞上》："易简而天下之理得矣。"《礼记·仲尼燕居》："礼也者，理也。"疏："理，谓道理，言礼者使万物合于道理也。"务（wù）：必须。事必当务，意谓办事知道先后缓急。长（cháng）：善，优。《孟子·公孙丑上》："'敢问夫子恶乎长？'曰：'我知言，我善养吾浩然之气。'"

【译文】

说话合理，办事知道缓急，这才是君子的长处，是一般人做不到的。

言有召禍也，行有招辱也

Heedless utterances may spell misfortune and disaster. Imprudent actions may beget disgrace and humiliation.

言有召祸也，行有招辱也。君子慎其所立乎！

《荀子·劝学》

Heedless utterances may spell misfortune and disaster. Imprudent actions may beget disgrace and humiliation. Therefore，gentlemen should be prudent with their words and actions.

【注释】

孔子主张慎言慎行，荀子也主张慎言慎行。《论语·为政》："子张学干禄，子曰：'多闻阙疑，慎言其余，则寡尤；多见阙殆，慎行其余，则寡悔。言寡尤，行寡悔，禄在其中矣。"**召、招**：王逸《楚辞》注："以手曰招，以言曰召。"召（zhào），呼唤。《诗经·小雅·出车》："召彼仆夫，谓之载矣。"招，以手示意，或用某种方式召之使来，引致。《尚书·说命下》："旁招俊乂。"《荀子·劝学》："登高而招，臂非加长也，而见者远。"立：设置。《易·说卦》："观变于阴阳而立卦。"《左传·桓公二年》："吾闻国家之立也，本大而末小，是以能固。故天子建国，诸侯立家。"

【译文】

说话不慎会招灾惹祸，行事不慎会遭受屈辱。所以君子要谨言慎行。

以善先人者，谓之教

Showing others good deeds is deemed teaching.

荀子说

以善先人者，谓之教；以善和人者，谓之顺。以不善先人者，谓之谄；以不善和人者，谓之谀。

《荀子·修身》

Showing others good deeds is deemed teaching; consenting to others with kindness is deemed amiableness. Showing others ill deeds is deemed insincerity; consenting to others with ill intentions is deemed flattery.

【注释】

荀子崇善，曰："伤良曰谗，害良曰贼。"孔子亦崇善，曰："三人行，必有我师焉。择其善者而从之，其不善者而改之。"（《论语·述而》）先：前导。《管子·形势》："道民之门，在上之所先。"注："上所先行，人必行之。"行动先于别人称先人。《左传·文公七年》："先人有夺人之心。"和（hè）：应和。《易·中孚》："鸣鹤在阴，其子和之。"《管子·白心》："人不倡不和。"顺：和顺。《诗经·郑风·女曰鸡鸣》："知子之顺之，杂佩以问之。"郑玄注："顺，谓与己和顺。"谄：奉承，献媚。《论语·学而》："贫而无谄，富而无骄。"谀：谄媚，用不实之词奉承人。

【译文】

用善良教人的，叫做教诲，用善良和人共事的，叫做顺理。用不善良教人的，叫做谄媚；用不善良和人共事的，叫做阿谀。

佚而治，约而详，不烦而功

Properly govern a state with ease; give simple yet well thought out orders; make achievements in state affairs without exertion.

佚而治，约而详，不烦而功，治之至也。

《荀子·强国》

Properly govern a state with ease; give simple yet well thought out orders; make achievements in state affairs without exertion. Such are the ideals of statesmanship.

【注释】

荀子游秦国，秦相范雎问他对秦国的印象如何，荀子对秦国的君臣、人民、形势地理基本上作了肯定的回答，后又说了这几句话。这可能是说秦虽强而不能统一天下的原因。**佚**（yì）：安乐。通"逸"。《庄子·大宗师》："夫大块载我以形，劳我以生，佚我以老，息我以死。"《孟子·尽心上》："以佚道使民，虽劳不怨。"**约**：简单，简略。《荀子·不苟》："（君子）总天下之要，治海内之众，若使一人。故操弥约而事弥大。"**详**：周备。《荀子·非相》："传者久则论略，近则论详。略则举大，详则举小。"**烦**：烦劳，相烦。《左传·僖公三十年》："若亡郑而有益于君，敢以烦执事。"**至**：极。《论语·雍也》："中庸之为德，其至矣乎！"《庄子·徐无鬼》："故海不辞东流，大之至也。"

【译文】

安闲而国家治理得很好，政令简约而周详，政务不烦乱而有功绩，这才是治国平天下的最高境界。

友者，所以相有也

Friends are those who hold affection for each other.

友者，所以相有也。道不同，何以相有也？

《荀子·大略》

Friends are those who hold affection for each other. How can those who have different principles and ambitions gain affection from each other?

【注释】

荀子曰："君人者不可以不慎取臣，匹夫不可以不慎取友。"**友**：古称同志为友。《周礼·地官·大司徒》："联朋友。"注："同师曰朋，同志曰友。同，犹齐也。"交友是儒家伦理道德的"五伦"之一。孔子提出"无友不如己者"（《论语·学而》），反对违心交友，"匿怨而友其人，左丘明耻之，丘亦耻之"（《论语·公冶长》），强调交友要有所选择，"益者三友，损者三友：友直、友谅、友多闻，益矣；友便辟、友善柔、友便佞，损矣"（《论语·季氏》）。**有**：亲爱，友爱。通"友"。《诗经·王风·葛藟》："谓他人母，亦莫我有。"《左传·昭公二十年》："若不获扞外役，是不有寡君也。"注："有，相亲有。"

【译文】

朋友，是相互友爱的。思想志向不相同的人，怎么能相互友爱呢？

有师法者，人之大宝也

Education and laws are the most precious treasures of the people.

有师法者，人之大宝也；无师法者，人之大殃也。人无师法，则隆性矣；有师法，则隆积矣。

《荀子·儒效》

Education and laws are the most precious treasures of the people; the absence of them is the worst disaster to affect the people. Without education and laws, people will indulge their natural propensity for evil; with them, people can prosper through achievement.

【注释】

师法：教育和法度。师，指（老师的）教育。法，法则，法度，规章。也指刑法，法律。《尚书·吕刑》："惟作五虐之刑于法。"荀子认为治国平天下仅靠礼乐是不够的，必须借助于刑法。这是荀子对儒家文化的发挥和发展。**大宝**：最珍贵的宝物。《易·系辞下》："圣人之大宝曰位。"后通称帝位为大宝。**殃**：灾祸。《尚书·伊训》："作不善，降之百殃。"**隆性**：助长本性的放纵。隆，助长。性，人的本性。《荀子·正名》："生之所以然者谓之性。"孟子认为人本性善良，而荀子则提出"人性本恶"的相对立的观点。**积**：功业。通"绩"。《荀子·礼论》："积厚者流泽广。"

【译文】

有教育和法度，是人最珍贵的宝物；没有教育和法度，是人最大的灾难。人如果没有教育和法度，就会助长恶的本性；有教育和法度，就能成就功业。

与人善言，暖于布帛

Kind words are as genial as warm clothes.

荀子说

与人善言，暖于布帛；伤人之言，深于矛戟。

《荀子·荣辱》

Kind words are as genial as warm clothes. Mean remarks are as hurtful as lance and halberd.

【注释】

荀子说："傲慢是人的灾祸；谦恭可以抵挡一切兵器。"**善言**：好话，有益的话。《孟子·离娄下》："禹恶旨酒而好善言。"《大戴礼记·子张问入官》："善言必听，详以失之。"**暖**：温暖。《礼记·王制》："七十非帛不暖，八十非人不暖。"**布帛**：丝、麻等织物的总称。《礼记·礼运》："治其麻丝，以为布帛。"**矛戟**：矛和戟都是长柄兵器，用以刺敌。

【译文】

对人说善良的话，让人感觉好像穿上棉衣一样温暖；对人说伤害的话，让人感觉像矛戟刺心一样痛。

乐者，圣人之所乐也

Music is what the sages favor.

乐者，圣人之所乐也，而可以善民心。其感人深，其移风俗易。故先王导之以礼乐，而民和睦。

《荀子·乐论》

Music is what the sages favor and it can shape the people. Music is powerful in influencing people and altering customs. Hence, the ancient sage kings employed music and rites to guide people and then they lived in harmony.

【注释】

这是荀子反对墨子的言论。墨子说："乐者，圣王之所非也；而儒者为之，过也。"荀子说："君子以为不然。"乐者，圣人之所乐也：音乐是圣人所喜爱的事物。前一个"乐"是音乐的意思。《易·豫》："先王以作乐崇德。"后一个"乐"（yào）是喜爱的意思。《论语·雍也》："知者乐水，仁者乐山。"善：改善。《易·渐》："山上有木，渐，君子以居贤德善俗。"疏："君子求贤，得使居位，化风俗使清善。"善俗，即移风易俗，使归于美善。《宋史·张载传》："（载）举进士，为祁州司法参军云岩令，政事以敦本善俗为先。"

【译文】

音乐，是圣人爱好的东西，而且可以用它改善民心。因为它感人深厚，且容易移风易俗。所以，先王用礼乐引导人民，人民因而能和睦相处。

乐者，乐也

Music is enjoyment.

乐者，乐也。君子乐其道，小人乐其欲。以道制欲，则乐而不乱；以欲忘道，则惑而不乐。

《荀子·乐论》

Music is enjoyment. Gentlemen seek truth and reason from such enjoyment whereas petty men seek to satisfy their worldly desires. Curbing desire with reason brings pleasure unaffected by debauchery. Disregarding reason due to sensual desires induces confusion rather than pleasure.

【注释】

荀子曰："乐者，治人之盛者也。而墨子非之。"乐者，乐也：前"乐"（yuè），音乐。后"乐"（lè），娱乐，愉快。君子乐其道，小人乐其欲：君子从娱乐中明白事理，小人从娱乐中满足情欲。道：规律，事理。《易·说卦》："是以立天之道曰阴与阳，立地之道曰柔与刚，立人之道曰仁与义。"《庄子·养生主》："庖丁释刀对曰：臣之所好者道也，进乎技矣。"欲，贪欲。包括物欲、情欲和色欲。《易·损》："君子以惩忿窒欲。"《素问·上古天真论》："以欲竭其精。"注："乐色曰欲。"乐而不乱：快乐而不淫乱。乱，淫秽行为。《荀子·天论》："男女淫乱。"惑而不乐：伤感而不快乐。感，伤。《广雅》："感，伤也。"

【译文】

音乐，就是娱乐。君子从娱乐中明白道理，小人从娱乐中满足情欲。用道理制止贪欲，就会快乐而不淫乱；如果为情欲而忘却道理，就会伤感而得不到快乐。

知莫大乎弃疑，行莫大乎无过

No wisdom is greater than the wisdom beyond bewilderment. No meritorious action exceeds the action beyond reproach.

知莫大乎弃疑，行莫大乎无过，事莫大乎无悔；事至无悔，而止矣。

《荀子·议兵》

No wisdom is greater than the wisdom beyond bewilderment. No meritorious action exceeds the action beyond reproach. No conduct outclasses the conduct free of compunction. Such conduct is the ultimate goal to be pursued.

【注释】

这是荀子和赵孝成王、临武君议兵时所谈的"为将之道"。他讲了这几句总括的话后，又说："六术、五权、三至，而处之以恭敬无圹，夫是之谓天下之将。则通于神明矣。"知（zhì）：同"智"。知、智古今字。《易·蹇》："见险而能止，知矣哉。"《论语·子罕》："择不处仁，焉得知。"行：行为。《论语·公冶长》："今吾于人也，听其言而观其行。"止：停止，停息。《易·艮》："时止则止，时行则行。"

【译文】

明智莫过于摒弃疑惑，行为莫过于没有过失，办事莫过于没有后悔。办事能做到不后悔，也就可以了。

志意修则骄富贵；道义重则轻王公

With a tempered will, one is able to shun power and wealth; holding one's principles dear, one can slight princes and aristocrats.

志意修则骄富贵；道义重则轻王公。内省外物轻矣。

《荀子·修身》

With a tempered will, one is able to shun power and wealth; holding the one's principles dear, one can slight princes and aristocrats. Scrutinizing one's inner self, one is able to shun worldly things.

【注释】

荀子重修身培养道德，这和孔子说"德之不修，学之不讲，闻义不能徙，不善不能改，是吾忧也"的意思大致相同。修：整治。《尚书·禹贡》："四海会同，六府孔修。"骄：高傲，傲慢。《论语·学而》："贫而无谄，富而无骄。"引申为轻视。内省（xǐng）：省察内在的自我。《论语·颜渊》："内省不疚，夫何忧何惧。"

【译文】

修炼心志就可以看轻荣华富贵；看重道义就可以轻视王公权贵。注重内在的自我省察就不以身外之物为重了。

自知者，不怨人；知命者，不怨天

Those who know their own limitations will not blame others; those who comprehend the course of fate will not blame Heaven.

198

荀子说

自知者，不怨人；知命者，不怨天。怨人者穷，怨天者无志。失之己，反之人，岂不迂乎哉？

《荀子·荣辱》

Those who know their own limitations will not blame others; those who comprehend the course of fate will not blame Heaven. Those who blame others will find themselves without resources in the end; those who blame Heaven are short in ambition. Though one has flaws, one still seeks them out in others. Isn't it a long path to take to find the truth?

【注释】

自知：自己了解自己。《老子》："知人者智，自知者明。" **知命**：知天命识穷达之分。《论语·尧曰》："不知命，无以为君子也。"疏："命谓穷达之分。" **穷**：终极。《荀子·富国》："纵欲而不穷，则民心奋而不可说也。" **失之己，反之人**：错误在自己身上，却在别人身上找原因。反，回，归还，通"返"。《左传·僖公二十三年》："楚子飨之曰：'公子若反晋国，何以报不毂？'"如果把"反"理解为"反省"，也通。**迂**（yū）：路远。

【译文】

有自知之明的人不会埋怨人，知道天命穷达的人不会埋怨天。埋怨人的人走投无路，埋怨天的人没有志气。错误在自己身上，却在别人身上找原因，这不是绕远了吗？

足国之道，节用裕民，而善臧其余

The approach to prospering a country lies in economic expenditure, enriching the people and the proper keeping of the surplus.

足国之道，节用裕民，而善臧其余。节用以礼，裕民以政。

《荀子·富国》

The approach to prospering a country lies in economic expenditure, enriching the people and the proper keeping of the surplus. Economize expenditure with the norm of etiquette; enrich the people with policies.

【注释】

荀子曰："不知节用裕民，则民贫；民贫则田瘠以秽；田瘠以秽则出食不半。上虽好取侵夺，犹将寡获也。"足：充实，足够。《诗经·小雅·信南山》："既霑既足，生我百谷。"《论语·颜渊》："子贡问政。子曰：'足食，足兵，民信之矣。'"节用：节省开支。《论语·学而》："敬事而信，节用而爱人，使民以时。"朱熹《集注》："易曰：'节以制度，不伤财，不害民！盖侈用则伤财，伤财必至于害民，故爱民必先于节用。'"裕民：使百姓富足。《国语·吴语》："裕其众庶，其民殷众，以多甲兵。"臧（cáng）：收藏。通"藏"。《汉书·食货志》"春耕夏耘，秋获冬臧。"裕民以政：以政令使民富足。孔子认为百姓富足是国家政权稳定的前提。故他说："百姓足，君孰与不足？百姓不足，君孰与足？"（《论语·颜渊》）孟子提出"明君制民之产必须仰足以事父母，俯足以畜妻子，乐岁终身饱，凶年免于死亡。"（《孟子·梁惠王上》）并说"无恒产者无恒心"（同上）。

【译文】

富国之道，应是节省开支而使百姓富足，并且要善于储存余财。用礼制节省开支，用政令使百姓富足。

201

责任编辑：韩　颖
英　译：张　乐
封面设计：胡　湖
印刷监制：佟汉冬

图书在版编目（CIP）数据

荀子说：汉英对照／蔡希勤编注．—北京：华语教学
出版社，2012
　（老人家说系列）
ISBN 978–7–5138–0142–3

Ⅰ.①荀…　Ⅱ.①蔡…　Ⅲ.①汉语—对外汉语教学—
自学参考资料②儒家—汉、英　Ⅳ.①H195.4②B222.6

中国版本图书馆 CIP 数据核字（2011）第 161630 号

老人家说·荀子说

蔡希勤　编注

*

ⓒ华语教学出版社
华语教学出版社出版
（中国北京百万庄大街 24 号　邮政编码 100037）
电话：(86)10- 68320585　68997826
传真：(86)10- 68997826　68326333
网址：www.sinolingua.com.cn
电子信箱：hyjx@sinolingua.com.cn
北京市松源印刷有限公司印刷
2012 年（大 32 开）第 1 版
（汉英）
ISBN 978–7–5138–0142–3
定价：35.00 元